Viva Britannia

By the same author

Eurocommunism: Myth or Reality?
(with Edward Mortimer and Jonathan Story)

Viva Britannia

Mrs Thatcher's Britain

Paolo Filo della Torre

SIDGWICK & JACKSON
LONDON

First published in Great Britain in 1985
by Sidgwick & Jackson Limited

Copyright © 1985 by Paolo Filo della Torre

ISBN 0–283–99143–7

Phototypeset by Falcon Graphic Art Ltd
Wallington, Surrey
Printed in Great Britain by
Biddles Limited, Guildford, Surrey
for Sidgwick & Jackson Limited
1 Tavistock Chambers, Bloomsbury Way
London WC1A 2SG

I would like to thank Martin Cole, Heather Weeks, Carolyn Coke, William Shawcross and Rosemary Spencer for their help.

Contents

— 1 —

Britain – old and new

An Italian in London invited an English girl out. When he took her home and said a polite goodnight she turned to him: 'You dress like an Englishman and you talk like an Englishman. You don't play the guitar. You don't sing. You don't make a pass at me. I'm not sure you're really Italian at all.'

The British have their stereotypes of foreigners, just as the world has its myths about the British. The difference, however, is that foreigners are fascinated by the British, whereas the British are quite unmoved by foreigners. J B Priestley observed: 'Europeans settling in England start thinking that the English are stupid, and then begin to wonder if these islanders are not really rather cunning and treacherous. But the English are neither stupid nor cleverer – only different.' There are, of course, a few exceptions.

One of the ways in which the British are different is in the amount of official interference they will tolerate. The Roman historian, Tacitus, writing nearly two thousand years ago, said: 'The Britons themselves submit to levies, tribute and the tasks laid upon them by the government, if they are not treated oppressively. Oppression they cannot bear, being reduced far enough to give obedience, but not yet far enough to be slaves.'

This emphasis on the freedom of the individual has

been a continuous thread throughout British history, from the Magna Carta to the Civil War, to the institution of a constitutional monarchy, the reform bills and the rise of trade unionism. Nothing infuriates the British citizen more than the suspicion that his privacy is being invaded by bureaucrats.

The planned introduction of a new system of national insurance cards provoked howls of outrage in Parliament and the press, with the suggestion that this might be the hidden introduction of a system of identity cards. Most foreigners, used to carrying identity cards since birth, failed to see what the fuss was about. But to an Englishman, his word is his bond and he sees no reason why he should produce official proof that he is indeed who he says he is.

Once an English lady showed me her passport to prove that the malicious gossip going round London about her age was quite untrue. I only allowed myself to read:

Her Britannic Majesty's Principal Secretary of State for Foreign and Commonwealth Affairs Requests and requires in the Name of Her Majesty all those whom it may concern to allow the bearer to pass freely without let or hindrance, and to afford the bearer such assistance and protection as may be necessary.

At that moment, I understood why the most republican of people choose to retain a monarch as head of state and representative to the rest of the world. 'There will soon be only five kings left, the kings of England, diamonds, clubs, hearts and spades,' said King Farouk bitterly after he had been driven into exile.

For over half a century it has been the wry joke of the

British that their royal family is thoroughly middle-class; a view which the Queen apparently shares, if her remark about the impending arrival of the new Princess Michael of Kent in the bosom of the family is correct: 'Oh dear, she is much too grand for us.' Not grand, and not even particularly British. Indeed it is hard to find a king or queen of England, since the Norman conquest, who could be said to be truly English. French satirist Pierre Daninos pointed out that the Plantagenets were French, the Tudors Welsh, and the Stuarts Scottish; they were followed by a Dutchman, who was succeeded by a German of the Hanoverian dynasty who spoke not a word of English. Despite this, the British monarchy has been accorded the full loyalty of its subjects almost without a break for one thousand years – and it is still the embodiment of the nation's essence. 'For Queen and country,' is no idle cry.

British soldiers do not believe in the Italian recommendation 'Make love not war'; they go enthusiastically into battle. Britons going into battle at whatever time and in whatever quarter of the globe have fought more tenaciously for the belief that they were defending the honour of the nation, personified in their monarch, than for any mere strategic interest. The present Queen Mother reciprocated this loyalty by staying in London with the King throughout the Blitz in the last war. The enormous affection in which the British people hold her stems as much as anything from her remark when Buckingham Palace was hit: 'I'm glad we have been bombed. Now I can look the East End in the face.'

Coming from Italy, a country where our experience of monarchies has been at best turbulent, I have been deeply impressed by the stabilizing influence of the British royal family. Far from being the standard-bearer of one or other faction, the Queen is the figurehead of all her people. The relaxed attitude her subjects appear to take towards her, which so surprises foreigners, is deceptive. The British, who can absorb any amount of left-wing oratory relatively unmoved, are quickly angered by criticism of the Queen. She sees her role as a job, more full-time than most, but nonetheless something she has contracted to do in return for the consent of her subjects to her reign.

Surprisingly for such a patriotic people, the British take an extraordinarily casual attitude towards their flag. Foreigners are taken aback to see it emblazoned on underpants, chocolate boxes and tawdry souvenirs. In Italy it is a criminal offence to show disrespect to the national flag. The Russian, American and French flags are totems of their respective political systems, but the British seem to have a curiously dual attitude towards the Union Jack (as the Union flag is popularly known). On the one hand it is taken entirely for granted and abased to the level of a cheap joke, and on the other hand it is capable of arousing the strongest patriotic emotion – one only needs to be present at the annual Remembrance Day ceremony at the Cenotaph in Whitehall to realize how deeply the English feel about what their flag represents.

It was not surprising that in the 1930s the Nazis should have regarded Britain with disdain; in the face of their rising militarism she must have appeared effete and spineless, so they made the arrogant mistake of under-estimating the strength of her principles. No true Britisher (as foreigners insist on calling them) would stand idly by while the playground bully beat up the weakest children. As Churchill warned von Ribbentrop: 'You must not underrate England, she is a curious country and very few foreigners can understand her mind . . . she is very clever. If you plunge us into another Great War, she will bring the whole world against you, like last time.' And so she did, and won – just as she had beaten Napoleon and was to beat Galtieri.

A hundred and fifty years ago the French statesman, Guizot, described England as 'the bulwark of freedom and human dignity'. 'Thanks to God and the Navy she has never been invaded,' quipped André Maurois, who himself had served in the British armed forces. No other European country has escaped the feet of an invading army, but centuries of inviolability have not made the British smug or careless. On the contrary, their fighting forces have recently proved their professionalism in real conflict, and the rest of the world, which at first laughed at the sight of British soldiers training for a comic opera war on the decks of ocean liners, choked back its derision when those soldiers yomped across boggy Falkland mountains in mid-winter and sent an Argentine army packing. Particularly remarkable to a foreigner in England in 1982 was the lack of ill-will shown by the British soldiers towards the Argentinians, even though their armies were fighting each other. They appeared to feel rather sorry for the young conscripts sent into action against them, who had been goaded into fighting to the last man by lurid stories of how the British ate their captives. British soldiers even went so far as to give up their own clothing and food to the frozen, terrified youngsters.

British pragmatism towards their former enemies has often surprised foreigners, but the British themselves see this as a common-sense acknowledgement of *realpolitik*. The Empire was largely built by the hardy mercantile Scots, while Wales has produced a stream of politicians whose Celtic passion and oratorical gifts enriched the proceedings of the House of Commons for centuries. In this century the British have respected (and, in some cases, even received at Buckingham Palace) men whom they had formerly considered terrorists: De Valera, Begin, Mahatma Gandhi and Pandit Nehru were all wanted men, as were the African leaders Kenyatta, Mugabe and Nkomo.

For centuries, refugees from political or economic turmoil overseas have traditionally found sanctuary in the British Isles, and many sectors of the British economy have flourished with the help of immigrant brains or brawn, as shown by the Flemish weavers' contribution to the textile industry in the fifteenth century, the construction by Irish labourers of the railway and canal systems which underpinned British industrial supremacy in the eighteenth and nineteenth centuries, and, perhaps of greatest fundamental significance, by the role played by the Jews in the financial activities of the City of London. The British press owes much of its vitality to the new-world dynamism of the American Astor and the Canadian barons, Beaverbrook and Thomson.

When I met the MP Sir Hugh Rossi for the first time, I expected to meet an ordinary Italian – his name being like Smith in Italy – so I was surprised to find an English gentleman of impeccable British outlook. Through him I discovered that foreigners wishing to settle here are inevitably absorbed into the British atmosphere and can even become more British than the British. An example is the Czechoslovakian-born Robert Maxwell, who was elected to the House of Commons for the Labour Party within eight years of arriving in this country and who went on to make a fortune in the typically British capitalist world of publishing. Other examples are Professors Kaldor and Balogh, who moulded a generation of economic thinkers, or Charles Forte, Arnold Weinstock and Michael Edwardes, whose entrepreneurial and managerial talents have made such an impact on British industry – all have become as British as have, for example, the thousands of Poles who fled to Britain during the Second World War. Charles Forte, Professors Kaldor and Balogh, and also Arnold Weinstock have had the supreme stamp of recognition bestowed upon them in the form of a life peerage, and are now entitled to put on the velvet and ermine robes of the House of Lords alongside scions of the most ancient families in the land.

The twin rocks on which this idiosyncratic society is founded are reverence for tradition and the right to free speech. George Mikes, a refugee from the Hungarian Communist régime, appreciated that democracy in Britain is a way of life as much as a system of government: 'In England it is bad manners to be clever, to assert something confidently. It may be your personal view that two and two make four, but you must not state it in a self-assured way, because this is a democratic country and others may be of a different opinion.' In 1902, the Communist Trotsky described an experience that could never have happened in his own country:

> One Sunday I went with Lenin and Krupskaya to a London church where a Social Democrat meeting alternated with hymn-singing. A compositor, who had returned from Australia, stood up and talked about the social revolution. Thereupon everyone got up and sang 'Almighty God, make it that there will be no more kings or rich people.' I could not believe my eyes or ears.

But Trotsky was as guilty of misjudging the British as Napoleon. No Englishman, of whatever class, would consent to being lumped together with 'the masses', and the barricades hold no attraction for these phlegmatic individualists, whose aspirations are all upper middle-class. Besides, my experience is that working-class solidarity is a myth here, because the different groups prefer to fight for their own interests. Revolutionary fervour passes them by. To them *liberté* means freedom from the intrusive power of the state, *égalité* means equality before the law, and as for *fraternité*, well, 'talk about pay with any British trade union official, and you will immediately hear the word "differentials",' as one MP says.

The proudest boast of the British must surely be the attraction that eminent men and women of all periods and from all countries have felt towards its way of life. Erasmus, mainspring of the Renaissance and inspiration of the profoundest intellectual turning-point in the last millenium, was himself inspired by the contemporary English mind: 'I never liked anything so much before. I find the climate both pleasant and wholesome, and I have met with so much kindness and so much learning . . . I can truly affirm that there is no entire country which has bred me so many friends, so sincere, so learned, so devoted, so brilliant, so distinguished by every kind of virtue as the single City of London.' When, more than two hundred years ago, Count Lichtenberg attended a debate in Parliament in 1770 he wrote afterwards: 'I could scarcely believe that such expressions were permitted in an assembly of this kind . . . It was vastly impressive and moving.'

Perhaps the supreme compliment to the quality of English minds was paid by Voltaire:

I know that England is a country where the arts are highly honoured and well rewarded, and where there may be a difference between the conditions of men, but no other difference exists except that of merit. It is a country where men think freely and nobly, without the restraint of any servile fear. If I followed my inclinations, I would settle here with the sole idea of learning how to think.

Truly, as Mr Ovchinnikov said, 'Money may be centred in New York, brothels in Paris, but ideals – ideals come from London alone.' This is the result of the glorious history of an aristocratic nation. The Pax Britannica is still an essential reference for historians.

Getting to know the British in the face of their massive indifference to foreigners seemed at first to present insuperable problems. To them an Italian was an opera singer, a waiter or a count. Fortunately I happen to be one of the few authentic specimens of the third category.

When I came to London as a journalist it was a far-off country, far not in distance but in customs and ideas; difficult and mysterious. For the first few days I thought: 'This venture is hopeless; I shall never get to know the people, never be able to communicate with them. The mixture of my bad English accent and the British lack of effort to understand foreigners is too much. The gulf is too wide.' But as André Maurois advised a young man going to England: 'Be reassured. The gulf can be crossed. Tell yourself that when the English have adopted you they will be your most faithful friends. Their friendship is worth making an effort to win.'

Arming myself with every possible guidebook to the British character, I set out to learn about this fascinating, inspiring and infuriating people. I even tried to learn about cricket, although every time I tried to play I was politely advised to retire and join the spectators. I found that, just as Jacob Rathgeb, the secretary to the Duke of

Wurttenburg, had in 1592, that: 'the inhabitants of London care little for foreigners. They scoff and laugh at them.' The chaplain to the Venetian ambassador to London in 1617–19, Orazio Busino, reported that: 'Foreigners are ill-regarded, not to say detested in London, so sensible people dress in the English fashion . . . and then mishaps are avoided.'

I assumed what I believed was an English appearance – I even bought myself a bowler hat. I decided to find out how the Englishman ate. More has been written about food and drink in Britain by foreign travellers than about any other aspect of English life and most of it is enough to daunt the courage of any new arrival. The adage that the only way to eat well in Britain was to have breakfast three times a day, was ignored, as was Francesco Caracciolo's 1750s remark that: 'There are in England sixty different religions and only one sauce.' Out went Pastor Moritz, with his verdict on what had obviously been an unpalatable gastronomic experience in 1782: 'An English dinner is half boiled or half roasted meat and a few cabbage leaves boiled in plain water on which they pour a sauce made of flour and butter.' But M. Moritz did find one dish worthy of praise: 'A kind of bread and butter which is toasted by the fire and is incomparably good; this is called Toast.' But I found little noticeable improvement in English coffee since Pastor Moritz's day: 'I would advise those who wish to drink coffee in England to mention how many cups are to be made with half an ounce, or else the people will bring them a prodigious quantity of brown water . . . ' In past centuries the British were noted for their spleen, which was often ascribed to their diet. 'They eat meat, meat and very little bread,' said Petrucci Ubaldini. 'Fresh fruit and vegetables play little part in their menus.'

The one appetite uniting City gentlemen in their clubs with factory workers in their canteens is a nostalgic preference for all those heavy dishes whose names alone can make a Continental blanch: cabinet pudding, treacle tart and bread-and-butter pudding are but foretastes of the delights in store, for the true Englishman can not do without his toad-in-the-hole, fly pie, spotted dick or dead man's leg. I even had to learn not to take offence when I heard that biscuits named after my distinguished compatriot, Garibaldi, were referred to in Britain as 'squashed flies'. It is the food of the nursery and prep school, of sub-Freudian comfort and contentment.

I soon discovered how to look for old-fashioned pubs, inns and restaurants. The growing interest in Continental cuisine has been paralleled by a decline in the popularity of English cooking. A recent survey revealed that English breakfasts were more easily obtained in Chicago than London. When English food can be had, it is now often of excellent quality. Steak and kidney pie can rightfully take its place among the great dishes of the world. Give me good red roast beef any time! The trouble starts when one is faced with a British translation of foreign cooking. Foreign dignitaries are always amazed to notice that the menus for banquets at Buckingham Palace are in French and that the royal cooks make admirable but vain efforts to imitate their legendary French counterparts. Fortunately those bastions of tradition, the London clubs, remain true to the old-fashioned fare that satisfied earlier generations.

My physical needs being catered for, I set out to investigate how the English lived. Like most foreigners, my idea of the British way of life had been moulded by P G Wodehouse, Nancy Mitford and J B Priestley, whose works far outsell those of other British authors

abroad. A late addition to the guide book library, the
Sloane Rangers' Handbook, has provided invaluable gui-
dance to the lifestyle of Bertie Wooster's female counterparts, and is now also (inexplicably) selling like hot cakes
in Continental bookshops.

I was agog to sample 'le style Anglais' in its native
habitat, but was quite unprepared for the discomfort
involved. Odette Keum was in no doubt as to the
miseries of English domestic arrangements when she
wrote in 1934 about the

> total absence of central heating, coal fires that warm
> about a square inch of space immediately in front of
> them, smoke from the coals until they are really lit,
> suffocation from that smoke and windows that must be
> left open whatever the weather may be, to counteract, by
> freezing, the asphyxiation induced by the smoke of the
> coal fires or the fumes of the gas fires.

No wonder that tweeds and cashmeres are even more
highly prized by foreigners accepting British hospitality
than they are by the natives themselves.

'The life of a country gentleman is what every Englishman dreams of and consciously or unconsciously takes as
his model. The English country gentleman is the highest
achievement of English civilization, the finest flower of
aristocratic culture.' This was the view of Cohen-
Portheim in 1930, although he drew the political moral
that, 'In order that the minority may have such a good
time, the majority must have a distinctly less good one.
The Englishman, with his governing-class ideal, is an
unconscious Nietzschean, but leaves open to everybody,
the possibility – and the hope – of rising to that class.'
And so the first acquisition of the successful British pop

star or boxer is a fine country house, even if he does find
the isolation too uncomfortable to spend much time in it.
Country living can plumb the depths of boredom as well
as the heights of civilization.

A foreigner cannot consider himself familiar with
British life until he has sampled that peculiarly British
phenomenon, the country house weekend. The perfect
description was produced by a native, A G MacDonell,
in 1956:

> If there is one social custom which distinguishes the
> Anglo-Saxon from the Latin, from the Slavonic, from the
> Basque, the Turanian and the Greek, it is the Saturday-
> to-Monday hospitality in the country. The Saturday-to-
> Monday period is invariably devoted to soul-searing
> self-analysis. It seemed that the English fin-de-semaine,
> when spent in sufficiently rural surroundings, was of an
> inspissated gloom, a tenebriferous melancholy, that
> made Strindberg's studies of demented lighthouse-
> keepers seem regular rollicks. Nothing ever happened
> except a fearful lot of heavy thinking and, from time to
> time, symbolical downpours of rain which gave scope for
> some beautiful English prose.

If his hosts do suggest some form of outdoor activity, the
foreigner will, as likely as not, find himself freezing to
death in some muddy field watching the junior members
of the family engaged in the horsy rituals of point-to-
point competition, running for hours across wild coun-
tryside in pursuit of hounds chasing some hapless fox or
hare, or trying desperately not to bring up his roast beef
lunch over the side of a sailing boat in water rough
enough to frighten the fish.

Returning to London after a weekend of acute physical
discomfort, redeemed only by his hosts' genuine

friendship and excellent port, the foreigner may be forgiven for asking himself why it should be that the English gentleman's lifestyle should have exerted such a visible influence on moneyed classes the world over. Is it that the qualities that made Britain great are thought to be synonymous with its rulers' pastimes? Are the concepts of fair play, team spirit and the cult of the English gentleman amateur inculcated on the playing fields of Eton, along with patriotism and principle? Why else would generations of world leaders send their children to be educated in English schools, or American tycoons seek to marry their daughters to English lords, or even, like William Waldorf Astor, to become one themselves?

Not all foreigners take a sympathetic view of the British, and some have found them pretty disagreeable: insular, 'a nation of shopkeepers', chauvinistic, obtuse and barbarous. And outstandingly contradictory, which I have seen illustrated by the Labour Party's vociferous condemnation of hunting (considered an upper-class sport on the anti-blood sports platform), while remaining strangely silent about angling, which is the working man's sport.

The British are unconcerned about their image abroad. Their challenge to the rest of the world is a sporting exercise, half for fun and half for real, and they often take a perverse delight in the insults thrown to them. To be an Old Contemptible was a badge of honour for veterans of what the Kaiser called 'a contemptible little army', in the Great War. They are free enough with their own insults in return: a headline last January when French farmers kidnapped lorryloads of British meat in protest at inadequate food prices proclaimed: 'The French are Revolting.' But for every visitor from abroad who has left these shores vowing never to return, many more have been attracted by what they have discovered to be a free, broadly tolerant society with deep reserves of principle and strength. After I had been here for a while I came to understand the subtlety of André Maurois' famous description of the English soul: 'like the English skies, the weather is nearly always bad, but the climate is good.'

The first requirement for an observer is not to draw attention to himself, which is easy enough in Britain where sartorial standards have set the international norm for decades. Marks and Spencer provided an excellent variety of perfect disguises although, in order to be served, I had to do battle in their Oxford Street store with elbow-shoving French, loud Americans and clucking trains of veiled Arab women, inevitably supervised by a solitary, uncomfortable man. I discovered Savile Row, Turnbull and Asser, Lobb and Lock. I quickly understood that dress is important in Britain, where the citizens have traditionally mistrusted and, on occasion, maltreated foreigners living in their midst who do not, for whatever reason, fit in. The upper classes would feel constrained in the presence of someone too obviously a foreigner, and would be unable to talk to him freely. The lower classes have traditionally made their antagonism clear in a somewhat more violent manner.

And indeed a number of continental observers attributed the criminal behaviour of the football hooligans at the Heysel Stadium and the notorious slaughter of Juventus supporters to the social and economic conditions of the citizens of Liverpool. But they were surprised to notice how well dressed so many of the hooligans were, and how much money they seemed to be spending, buying their tickets to the stadium at black market prices.

No, the British fans' dreadful behaviour had nothing to do with the lack of pounds in their pockets, but much more to do with their naturally aggressive mentality. Sophisticated Britons see things in a different light – they do not dislike foreigners as long as they do not overplay their role and create a disturbance. The British way of life must prevail, for Englishmen 'cannot get out of their skin, although it is a solid, and in every respect, an excellent skin' (Capek). Good manners dictate that voices are never raised, a habit which is especially trying for the Latin or Slavonic temperament. Neither is it done to display interest in an Englishman's personal life or, for that matter, to talk about your own. 'If you insist on making confidences they will be listened to with polite indifference . . . there is no middle course between silence and scandal. Choose silence' (Maurois again). But ask an Englishman for help and he will go far beyond the call of duty to respond. Ovchinnikov describes his discovery of how to break the ice on a long train journey:

> Attempts to engage strangers in conversation . . . are likely to prove fruitless (and particularly so if you begin by asking them the usual questions as to where they are going and why, whether they have children, or how much they earn) . . . You must begin by declaring your helplessness, by emitting, as it were, a distress signal which the English character is powerless to ignore. 'Excuse me please, but I'm a foreigner and I don't know very much about British politics. I wonder if you could explain to me why Scotland is talking of devolution?' After such a question your silent travelling companion is likely to launch into a two-hour lecture rather than just a simple answer. And it will by typified not only by its factual accuracy and seriousness of argumentation, but also by its unprejudiced, balanced account of all the various points of view on the given problem.

I have always been fascinated by the size and the legends of the British Empire, by the involvement of this country in teaching the rest of the world how to run a modern state, based on parliamentary democracy. In every former British territory, including the United States of America, I have been very much impressed by the efficiency, the civilized manners and the sense of law and order. I am still impressed by the pre-war geographical maps of the world, largely coloured in pink, which signified that the Union Jack was still waving in all the corners of the hemisphere. The splendour and the glory of the British Empire were the result of the efforts of a great nation and of great leaders. Reading about Elizabeth I, Queen Victoria, Palmerston, Nelson, Wellington, Disraeli, Cecil Rhodes and Winston Churchill has always been most interesting for me. I was told that, after the war, the chapter of greatness in the history of Great Britain was closed. I heard people echoing Dean Acheson – 'Britain, having lost her imperial role, has not yet found a new one.' For three decades this assumption seemed to be correct. Britain lost the Empire, paid very highly for her war effort against the Nazis and lost much of her wealth while other nations in the world became richer and more powerful. Yet this country rightly refused to relinquish her 'Englishness' and her people also refused to become just 'Europeans' like the other nations in Europe.

In Victorian times there were snobs little and large at every level of British society as the gradual encroachment of the industrial revolution loosened the framework of the old social order, bringing new wealth to many and creating a new class of urban poor. Today there is a new class of social rejects in the form of over three million unemployed people who either cannot or do not want to find work. And at the same time there is a flowering of snobbery in British society, exemplified by fashionable groups like the Sloane Rangers and Young Fogeys. The Italian historian Giovanni Battista Vico propagated the theory of the 'corsi e ricorsi storici' (the way history repeats itself). Although it has been disputed as a theory there is no doubt that foreign observers are much struck by present-day parallels with the Victorian age.

The 'Age of Improvement' means precisely this – that once again the middle classes and their values are not only running the country but, in a deeper sense, dictating the very style that the nation is beginning to adopt. And along with the rise of the middle classes, the old order is changing with the meritocracy replacing the Old School Tie. Under the banner of efficiency Mrs Thatcher is transforming the country. The historians say that the reign of Queen Victoria never succeeded in turning Britain into a true business society; Margaret Thatcher is now succeeding in doing so. There are three outstanding examples of Mrs Thatcher's success in propagating the value of work and material possessions: the sale of council houses which has turned millions of former tenants into home owners, the privatization of British Telecom which has made so many people shareholders for the first time, and the advent of over three million unemployed, which, by contrast, has made the rest of the population regard even unrewarding, badly paid jobs in a new light.

In Tommaso di Lampedusa's masterpiece *The Leopard*, Prince Salina says 'Bisogna che tutto cambi, in modo che niente cambi' (everything must change so that nothing changes). Mrs Thatcher's social revolution is not so much a threat to the existence of the hallowed British establishment as it is a threat to some of those who inhabit it. The accents of Eton and Oxford are becoming rarer in the Houses of Parliament, in the Church of England, at *The Times* and at the BBC, to such an extent that the elegant and quintessentially British political commentator Peregrine Worsthorne complains about the lack of old Etonians in the British Cabinet (there are, in fact, four at present). The new trend of Tory politicians is epitomized by Norman Tebbit, widely predicted to succeed Margaret Thatcher as leader of the Conservative Party, who is, like her, grammar school educated, but who, unlike her, has retained his original accent (in his case, from the London suburbs). Having qualified as a pilot in the RAF, the least 'fashionable' of the services, he spent seventeen years as a civil airline pilot before entering the House of Commons.

The *hoi polloi* are taking over with a mission: to put the punch back into the economy and, of course, to get richer themselves. It was, of course, Norman Tebbit, as Minister of Employment, who claimed that his father, in an earlier period of high unemployment unrelieved by today's social welfare provision, had 'got on his bike' to look for work – a political point whose insensitivity to present-day problems rather embarrassed his party.

The difference from the pre-Thatcher era of Harold Macmillan is quite impressive. Conservative Members of Parliament these days tend to marry their secretaries rather than the daughters of earls or dukes, especially the second time round, and those who, as sons of peers, are entitled to the appellation 'The Hon.' tend to suppress it. There is, however, still a good deal of snobbery around. Even if the *ancien régime* is being slowly replaced, it remains enough of a presence in the higher echelons of power to be deferred to and, on occasion, looked up to. Lord Carrington, as Foreign Secretary, was rumoured to

have been the only member of the Cabinet able to
dispute the Prime Minister's views with impunity – and
to have been listened to.

Against the Dallas-style vulgarity that is now a part of
Britain it is still possible to set the image of the House of
Lords, Royal Ascot and Henley, the garden parties at
Buckingham Palace and, of course, the Princess of
Wales's new hats. The symbols of tradition are still
there, respected and defended at great length. Every day
the continuing saga of the moneyed classes is retailed in
the columns of Nigel Dempster or William Hickey, and
the up-and-coming generation go to dancing lessons,
riding lessons, shooting lessons and even elocution lessons. The old upper crust may have been more cultured,
amusing, detached, frivolous and lovable, but the new
masters are stronger, more determined, whole-hearted
and ruthless.

The difference between the real members of the old
guard and those who merely mimic them is often difficult
to see; it may, indeed, be invisible to all but the most
sophisticated foreigners. The best that the American,
Japanese or European can do today in London is to buy
a house in Eaton Square, Chelsea and Kensington or
thereabouts, furnish it like an English castle and install
at least one Golden Retriever or Great Dane to lie by the
hearth. The 'in' foreigner will have an English wife and
an English horse and will send his children to one of the
'factories for gentlemen' – the English public schools.

This imitation of the English is not exclusively a rich
man's game. Continental plumbers still use pipes and
valves whose diameter is calculated in inches and frac-
tions of inches because when the former were exported
from Britain, naturally the latter had to fit. No system
could then abandon the old imperial measurements.

Some of the continental railways still run on the left. More and more often, especially in Europe, old-fashioned cafés are called pubs. English tweeds, pipes, brogues and hats are not the exclusive preserve of the British upper crust; many more working-class people now adopt these fashions and Americans have hijacked the plaid for everything from trousers to underwear. In the sixties the young would follow the lead set by the Beatles, Mary Quant, Carnaby Street and the King's Road, but now fashion is universally inspired by Princess Diana. This, in no small measure, is why British designers have had such international success.

For the foreigner, Mrs Thatcher's Britain projects a mixed image but still one that is unmistakeably alluring. Millions of tourists flood the shops and streets. They buy all the tea, whisky, cashmere, shoes and Jaguars in sight. So much shopping is done in the English high street that it is even difficult sometimes to find anything to export. Americans, Arabs and Europeans in London are prepared to pay a million pounds or more for a single house or a thousand pounds a week to rent a flat. Foreigners know that they can find any luxury they want in Britain: not only the best roast beef, smoked salmon or steak and kidney pie, but also the best caviar and vodka and the cheapest fine champagne. Now Britain exports spaghetti to Italy, wine to France and sausages to Germany; it is a sign that some of the British sense of enterprise, so much admired in past centuries by people like de Tocqueville and Voltaire, is just as strong as ever.

Until the beginning of this century Great Britain was arguably the leading country in the world: a large part of the atlas was pink, the colour of the British Empire. This is not the case today, of course. However, British men and women are still confident. They know that 'Britons never will be slaves', and, ostrich-like, they still look at the future with the sanguine eyes of a master race.

There is a great debate as to whether Mrs Thatcher's Britain is more the land of the Sloane Rangers or whether she has transformed the United Kingdom into a sort of Yuppies Land of American-style Young Urban Professionals. There is not a more determined public defender of the monarchy, the aristocracy, the public schools and Oxbridge than the Iron Lady herself, though her true allegiance seems to be to big business rather than to the civilized, non-materialistic aspects of traditional aristocratic values. The 'new Conservatives', therefore, are motivated primarily by ambition and greed, and some can fairly be said to be boorish, arrogant, vulgar, insensitive and callous, displaying their status and their money-making successes in a crude fashion. They are very different from the image that foreigners have of the 'English gentleman', who keeps a low profile, has good manners, a cultured lifestyle and civilized attitudes, has a deep attachment to the land and rural life, tends towards 'understatement', and never shows appreciation for anything which looks shiny and expensive.

The great interest in Young Aspiring Professionals (Yaps, also sometimes called Young Upwardly Mobile People – the Yumpies) is just something of the moment. They spread over Britain in the early seventies. They are part of the phenomenon dealt with by Samuel Brittan in his book *Capitalism and the Permissive Society*. The Yap has, according to Pearson Philip's book, *The Complete Guide to Young Aspiring Professionals*, 'a smooth boyish face, but showing lines of strain. It is difficult to guess his nationality just by looking at him. He has acquired bland, middle-Atlantic mannerisms. He has a tan in mid-winter.' Carlo Rossella, the most authoritative of the Italian travel correspondents, says, 'The Yaps are trying to import into Europe a sort of American life-style, a new language, a new culture. Is this new fashion compatible with civilisation? The vulgarity of the Yaps, their lack of good taste and appreciation of the classic pleasures of life make them alien characters.'

But Thackeray was proved to be right when he assumed that the British are as snobbish as the Greek gods. Even the 'nouveau anglais' secretly dreams of climbing the steps of the temple of the establishment, and once he has done so he may become so intransigent a defender of it that he may even forgo financial gain to preserve the sacred cows.

There are plenty of examples of anti-government revolts by the members of the House of Lords, the Church of England, the academic world, the Royal Navy, British industry and even the Conservative Party itself. These people ignore the most important basic factor: that Mrs Thatcher is the most determined advocate for the survival and the strengthening of the great British institutions, which she sees as contributing to Conservative legitimation and public docility. The Labour Party and some Liberals and Conservatives would like to abolish the House of Lords and replace it with an elected European-style second chamber, but the Prime Minister is determined to save the magical, talismanic heritage of the Upper House. The opposition parties (and some progressive Tories) would like to bring down Oxbridge to the level of other universities; Mrs Thatcher is not only an Oxford girl herself but she is also linked to the upper echelon of the academic world. Similar considerations may also be applied to the Royal Navy. If it is true that the defence structures of the

United Kingdom had to be adjusted to the nuclear age, it is also true that under the Iron Lady, the Royal Navy has regained its most glorious image; moreover the so-called nuclear deterrent, the most powerful weapon of the British defence armament, has been allocated to the Navy. Admirals and other members of the Navy who complain about this government's policies appear to overlook reality.

Another example of nonsensical moaning comes from the Confederation of British Industry, which complains when the pound goes down because it claims that it has to pay more for imports of machines and raw materials, and then complains even more bitterly when the pound goes up because, it says, British export prices are no longer competitive! British industrialists also tend to overlook the fact that under the present government their profits have been higher than during any previous period recently.

Some of the most striking revolts against Thatcher, because they are revolts by those who might be expected to stay loyal to the bitter end, are those coming from the Church of England and the Wet Conservatives. In the old days it was often said that the Church of England was the Conservative Party at prayer. Now that the Conservative Party has moved so far to the right, the Church of England seems to be more like the Social Democratic Party at prayer. Bishops, archdeacons and canons perhaps overlook the similarity of Mrs Thatcher's attitudes to traditional religious values of the last century – her view of crime as an individual aberration without social context, and her commitment to conventional family life as a power for social conservatism and compliance.

Never in the past have the Tories been led with such

success by one of their leaders, at least since the Falklands war ignited the dormant loyalties of the British public. Her triumphs and the considerable increase in the number of Conservative seats in 1983 are all due, as has been recognized by commentators all over the world, to 'the Thatcher factor'.

A National Consumer Council survey published in 1981 said that standards of service provided by many of the nationalized industries were clearly falling short of customers' expectations, leading to a pervasive discontent with declining standards. Many respondents expressed the view that they were captive customers – prices rose as standards dropped and there was little that they could do to reverse the trend. The overall performance of the major nationalized industries was extensively reviewed in an academic study published in 1981. The author, Richard Fryke, previously an enthusiast for nationalized industries, concluded the following:

> Although the picture is not wholly black, most of the industries display serious inefficiency because they do not use the minimum quantities of labour and capital to produce the goods and services that they provide. Furthermore, resources are being misallocated because of the widespread failure to pursue the optimum policies for pricing and production. Far too many of the nationalised industries produce at a loss, engage in average cost pricing or practise cross-subsidisation. In general, the nationalised industries' performance has been third rate though with some evidence here and there of first-class standards.

Mrs Thatcher's Britain seems not only to have succeeded in satisfying the traditional British entrepreneurial sense but it has also created the conditions for a new and more efficient economic system.

Some forty years ago, at the 1946 Conservative Party Conference, Sir Anthony Eden first defined the Tory alternative to the socialist state, supposedly created by Clement Attlee's government, as 'the creation of a nation-wide property-owning democracy'. Winston Churchill gave his blessing to the idea but the Conservative governments of Harold Macmillan and Edward Heath never really managed to achieve much progress towards creating a free market economy system in this country. To the great surprise of the whole world the Conservative government of Edward Heath added to the list of industries already nationalized the name of Rolls Royce, considered by foreigners as one of the symbols of 'the best of Britain'.

Now it is frequently asserted that, as well as improved efficiency, privatization offers another opportunity – that of increasing the spread of wealth through the encouragement of personal shareholding. By selling shares in state assets to the public, Thatcher's government has deliberately sought to encourage the individual investor, and in particular those who work for the companies concerned.

The British example of privatization has begun to be followed abroad. In Italy most of the state control on the food industry has been relinquished and this has been taken over by Signor Carlo de Benedetti, while the state oil company ENI floated its shares on the Italian stock exchange so that private capital and private involvement would be able to play a prominent part in this corporation. In France, socialist President François Mitterrand, who started his administration with a huge programme of nationalization, has been seduced by the capitalistic

songs of the Iron Lady; the gigantic, recently nationalized company Saint Gobain will be given back to the
private sector. In Japan the government-controlled Nip-
pon Telegraph and Telephone will be sold on the stock
exchange and so will the state railways. German government disengagement from the business world is also
considerable; public shareholding in the Volkswagen car
company is to be reduced by 14 per cent, in the Viag
aluminium company by 25 per cent, and in the oil
company Praklaseismos by as much as 50 per cent.

The Labour Party believed that nationalization would
engender a sense of identification among workers with
their company and give them a feeling of involvement in
its success. While the Conservative Party's objective of
privatization is now being seen as right, events have
shown that its past methods were entirely wrong. It
seems that the only way to achieve business efficiency is
by giving the workforce a personal financial stake in their
company, and it is for this reason that the Conservatives
have given special incentives to encourage employees to
purchase shares when an industry has been transferred
into the private sector, and in some cases has created
share bonus schemes for employees. At British Aeros-
pace the government offered each employee £50 worth of
shares to be held in trust for a minimum of two years, as
well as a promise to match each share bought and placed
in trust with a fee share to a maximum of sixty, and as a
result three-quarters of the eligible workforce took up
shares in the company. At Associated British Ports, 91
per cent of the workforce took up shares while the figure
at Amersham International and Cable and Wireless was
99 per cent in each case. The National Freight Corporation was actually sold to a consortium of its own
management and workforce with 82·5 per cent of the

issued share capital being initially held by employees and pensioners of the company. Wherever possible, priority has always been given to encourage employees to purchase shares in the enterprise.

The flotation of British Telecom, a business with a turnover of £6¾ billion and almost a quarter of a million employees, was the largest ever attempted on any stock exchange anywhere in the world. Once again, the government gave special incentives to the employees of the company to acquire shares. Not only will the result of this be that BT is in real public ownership – owned by the public and not the state – but it has given many people their first taste of capitalism by giving them a financial stake in a national enterprise. Money-making has again become a legitimate aspiration and people no longer expect to be spoon-fed. Like Queen Victoria, Mrs Thatcher has made people face up to the Darwinian law of survival of the fittest and the weakest to the wall.

According to the former financial editor of the *Guardian*, William Davis, a self-made millionaire himself from his publishing interests, there are 4,000 millionaires in Britain divided into four main categories:

Rich: £1 million to £5 million
Very rich: £5 million to £20 million
Super rich: over £20 million to £30 million
Can't count: any family worth more than £35 million.

The main difference that impresses any onlooker is the fact that whereas the old-fashioned millionaires were quite invisible, the Thatcher tycoons are very much in evidence.

Foreigners have always been amazed by the differences between the classes and these differences have, in the past, often been blamed for the unsatisfactory British industrial performance during this century. But from my own personal experience I have noticed that, contrary to the fascinating theses of Jilly Cooper, this profound 'class distinction' is not as profound as it looks. Really the important aim of any social class seems to be to try and climb a rung or more up the social ladder. My friends from the working classes seem to be determined to look as if they are middle-class, the middle classes try to look like aristocrats and the aristocrats try to look like royalty. This attitude might be thought very snobbish, but I am always amazed at how foreigners keep on imitating the British middle classes and even the British aristocracy.

Attempts to launch a class war have failed disastrously. Karl Marx predicted a revolution in Britain because he thought that the British proletariat resented being exploited, but in reality British democracy is too strongly established to be overthrown by revolution. Marxism cannot succeed here because it is based on class solidarity, and in Britain the working class is too fragmented and individualistic, as well as too patriotic, to make a revolution. There is a sense of history that makes any citizen of the United Kingdom feel that he is better than the people on the other side of the Channel. This sense of national identity may be jingoistic, it may be selfish, but it is there. People seem prepared to make sacrifices for the good of the nation. At the same time they do not seem to be interested in egalitarianism either on an international or on a national basis.

Harold Wilson, when he tried to rally the nation, evoked the 'spirit of Dunkirk'; Mrs Thatcher can more easily call on the nationalistic spirit of the Falklands war. But she can also appeal to the British people's individual ambition and to British snobbery that makes everybody determined to climb the social ladder. Anthony Wedgwood Benn may be convincing, an erudite demagogue who claims to speak for the working classes when he promotes an egalitarian society, but the British 'poor' do not follow his argument and they do not aim at egalitarianism. They aim at improving their income and their social status.

People call the phenomenon of 1979, the rise of the grocer's daughter from Grantham, 'Thatcherism', as if it were all her doing. In reality, of course, it is the great wheel of history turning behind the scenes. This is what caused her astonishing rise. Mrs Thatcher, from her humble background, fully understands what rich, left-wing theoreticians never understand: egalitarian aspirations have never been part of working-class culture. People do not want to be equal to their neighbour – they want to be more affluent than their neighbour. The first step the new owner of a former council house takes is to alter its external appearance in some way to differentiate it from the homes of his tenant neighbours. Maggie has created a Britain where hard work, risk and imagination really can pay.

— 2 —

The most exciting country in Europe

My residence in London has, more or less, coincided with Mrs Thatcher's rise to prominence, but my earliest experience of British politics occurred long before that, when the Italian newspaper, *24 Ore*, asked me to cover the 1961 Conservative Party Conference.

To a foreigner, Britain in the late 1950s and early 1960s was the most exciting country in Europe. The end of post-war reconstruction was celebrated by the magnificent state visit of the Queen and the Duke of Edinburgh to Paris in 1956, when the most sophisticated city in the world gave itself over to honour the young couple. The British were confidently looking forward to a revival of their old prosperity, with the added benefits of their welfare state – 'the envy of the world' – which would ensure that all levels of society would participate in the spoils. 'You never had it so good' summed up the national mood after three decades of depression, conflict and austerity. Throughout Europe, Britain was the focus of enormous goodwill in memory of her wartime courage, and her cheerful optimism attracted hordes of foreigners to taste the fruits of her success. Few people then realized that these fruits were the last good yield from a debilitated stock, that this was but a spasm in the long slow

decline of Britain's economic power, and that her place
in the world had irremediably shifted from the first to the
second league of nations.

In 1961, however, the Macmillan government was
riding high, and the Conservative Party Conference of
that year was billed as an historic event when Britain
would announce its decision to join the European Community. Naturally, the foreign media were interested.
Macmillan appeared to be achieving the impossible: he
was persuading the British to turn their minds from the
past glories of the Empire to the future uncertainties of
partnership in a European enterprise. In contrast to the
bitterness felt by the Italians and the French at the loss of
their African colonies, Britain under Macmillan seemed
to be adopting a pragmatic attitude of withdrawal with
the aim of maintaining British influence, and particularly British economic interests, in her former colonies,
rather than risk losing everything by hanging on too
long. What impressed foreigners from more turbulent
political backgrounds was the stability that Macmillan
maintained while bringing about such revolutionary
changes. He managed this partly by surrounding himself
with members of the traditional ruling caste so that the
illusion of continuity was retained, and by managing a
consumer boom which occupied people's energies in the
pursuit of prosperity – understandable at that time.

'Britain was never so rich as when she had off-loaded
her Empire,' says Anthony Sampson in his *Changing
Anatomy of Britain*, yet underneath it all Macmillan
shared with other serious politicians of his generation the
awareness of 'the special dangers of a nation in the
aftermath of Empire and industrial supremacy: they had
to steer it from the wider seas of world domination into
the narrower waters of national competition and co-

operation with neighbours'. Tragically for Britain, Macmillan's attempt to enter the Common Market in 1961 came to grief on the rocks of General de Gaulle's suspicion and pride. It is interesting to speculate on the subsequent development of the Conservative Party had Britain been accepted into the Community at the outset: without General de Gaulle would there have been a Mrs Thatcher? Once inside the Community, would Britain have found it easier to adjust its own social and industrial structures to the changed commercial imperatives of the world than it did when it was eventually accepted as a member ten years later?

None of the difficulties that lay ahead were suspected at Llandudno in October 1961. Macmillan's speech to the Party Conference was eloquent and convincing, his choice of words perfect, his arguments unchallengeable. For me this was an impressive first taste of British political party conferences.

It was another Conservative Party Conference that brought me back to Britain two years later for what promised to be a climactic occasion for the party. Macmillan was a sick man, and his future as leader of the party was in doubt. Moreover, his record as Prime Minister was now seen to be notable for bluff rather than substance: in effect he had been over-optimistic when he promised the people of Britain that all was going to be for the best in the best of all possible worlds, while concealing the lamentable truth about the rate at which they were falling behind their competitors abroad. His European policies had not worked out, and although he could not be held responsible for General de Gaulle's prickly sensitivity towards the British, he betrayed his un-European outlook by failing to appreciate how the Europeans, and particularly the French, would view

Britain's strong attachment to the American relationship. On the domestic front his unwillingness to
grasp the nettle of Britain's economic problems had left
the way open for the trade unions to increase their
influence in proportion, it seemed, to their lack of
justification for doing so. The resulting split between the
left and right wings of the Conservative Party was
inevitably going to make the battle for the succession
that much sharper, and reveal to the world what was
really going on inside the soul of the British governing
party.

Foreign newspapers had in any case recently been
devoting untold column-inches to lurid accounts of the
Profumo scandal, and were eager for more insights into
the strange character of the British male, evidently so
passionate under his phlegmatic exterior. As the Abbé
Blanc observed centuries ago:

> The English seem to fear the company of women as
> much as the French delight in it – they think the fair sex
> are made only to take possession of their hearts, and
> seldom or never to afford any amusement to their minds.
> They prefer the pleasure of toasting their healths in a
> tavern to that of chatting with them in a circle.

Indeed, the British propensity for getting into a mess
over sex never ceases to amaze and often amuse foreigners, especially natives of my country. Is it a result of
the public school ethos, with its emphasis on discomfort,
male solidarity and deprivation of female influence,
together with the concomitant view that the delights of
the flesh must be sinful? Or is it simply the fate that
attends him who breaks the eleventh commandment,
'Thou shalt not be found out'? When the entire world

started to appreciate the effect that Christine Keeler had had on the British ruling classes, the political and social analysis of the British scene changed dramatically. Until then we foreigners had believed that the British were a people obsessed by bigotry. Most of my European friends believed, up until 1963, that the British were so puritanical that they even covered piano legs.

Llandudno had done nothing to prepare me for the culture shock in store for every first-time overseas visitor to Blackpool: the cold, the discomfort, above all the unbelievable kitsch. Raincoats flapping around the knees of politicians, party activists and journalists as they fought their way along the prom into the teeth of a nor'wester; trams dressed overall as sputniks or steamships, clanking past the rows of dismal hotels where elderly couples sat immobile behind huge glass windows gazing out over the heaving grey sea, like goldfish mesmerized by the sight of their native element in its wild state; decorative lights, on which no expense had been spared to raise them to the zenith of vulgarity, dancing crazily as the wind screamed through their overhead wires; all combined to create a fascinating nightmare redeemed, it must be said, by the inhabitants' warm welcome and hearty appetite for food, drink and hilarity.

No sooner had the conference begun than its proceedings were completely disrupted by the news of Macmillan's illness, and it became clear that he would be unable to carry on. The drama of the succession gained momentum against the – to me – wildly inappropriate setting for a political conference, the red plush seats and potted palms of the Winter Gardens, the after six taffeta and tulle and dinner jackets of the delegates, the dinners, the dances, the glitter and laughter, with little evident politicking, were all so different from an Italian political conference – or from a Labour one, for that matter! When later on I attended Labour Party Conferences I was struck by the equivalent role-playing on the opposite side of the political spectrum: the women aping Virginia Woolf, the men in tweeds and heavy glasses poisoning the air with their pipes, the atmosphere vibrant with Fabian intellectualism; the whole conference, as Oscar Wilde might have observed, gone a-Bloomsburying. The modern Labour Party is redder in tooth and claw than the Conservatives have traditionally been, but both parties do their real fighting away from the public gaze. Smoke-filled rooms exist in Blackpool and Brighton, Llandudno and London, but what goes on inside them is shrouded in secrecy. Remembering the old jibe about the Church of England being the Conservative Party at prayer, I am tempted to substitute 'politics' for 'church' in Ronald Blythe's remark, 'As for the British Churchman, he goes to church as he goes to the bathroom, with the minimum of fuss and no explanation if he can help it.'

The battle for the succession to Macmillan was fought out behind closed doors. In the end the extraordinary English concept of 'the old school tie' bound the kingmakers into a magic circle: eight out of the nine men charged with sounding out opinion in the party had been to Eton, and those contenders who had not had that privilege started at a disadvantage in the light of Macmillan's well-known preference for men of his own background. Although the final decision was not taken until a week later, the Party Conference naturally provided the opportunity for each contender to test his support. As the acting leader of the party, Butler decided to try and keep the temperature down by carrying out

Macmillan's engagements, but on the Thursday evening he had the misfortune to be walking through the foyer of the Winter Gardens (escorted by two detectives) on his way from one party to another, just as the excited audience was spilling out of the CPC meeting at which Hailsham had declared he would renounce his peerage in order to stand as a candidate for the leadership. The reserved RAB must have found Hailsham's ebullient supporters unpalatable, and in any case the jockeying had already begun back at the Imperial Hotel. The entire press corps had jammed the hotel lobby, studying every expression on every passing minister's face in the heat and glare of the lights needed by the enormous old-fashioned television cameras. I remember Gerald Scarfe sitting on the floor making lightning sketches of politicians as they fought their way through the crush, while Robin Day stood nearby in a position to catch the most discreetly whispered innuendo.

Everything and nothing was settled at Blackpool. I returned to Italy at the end of the week as much in the dark as everyone else as to who Macmillan's successor would be, although indications had been present in Home's measured winding-up speech to the conference which contrasted strongly with Hailsham's excitability in front of the cameras. Sir Alec Douglas-Home, as he became, presented a small problem to foreign observers, for the complex rules governing the use of titles and Britain's attitude towards its politician peers seemed both unintelligible and archaic. He soon appeared vulnerable in a country undergoing dramatic social changes, though he impressed many foreigners with his simplicity and integrity. But however estimable these qualities may have been, they were no match for the cunning tactician Douglas-Home had to face across the

despatch box. A year later he lost the general election to
Harold Wilson, and a year after that, having failed to
unite the party behind him, he lost its confidence and
was obliged to give way to a Conservative from a vastly
different background, Edward Heath.

The Macmillan years were undoubtedly exciting and
affluent, but in many ways they were far from the British
economic reality. With hindsight it is clear that many of
the difficulties facing Britain in the 1970s were already
emerging under Macmillan's premiership. The consumer society, with its safety net in the welfare state, became
a society of individuals looking to the state to provide for
every need. The consumer boom and expansionist economic policies led inexorably to the inflation which brought
the British economy to its knees by the mid-1970s.
Policies undertaken with the highest intentions developed into travesties of themselves. Higher education
for all has, in practice, degenerated into lower education
for all. The economic improvement benefited everybody
but most of the wealth went into consumer spending,
with the result that investment and efficiency were
sacrificed to satisfy the demand for cars, refrigerators,
television sets and new clothes.

The extraordinary thing is that despite widespread
agreement about the long-term negative consequences of
Macmillan's rule, the English have now, twenty years
on, acknowledged the stamp he left on his era by
elevating him to the House of Lords. To a foreigner this
looks like a straightforward reward for longevity; a more
charitable explanation could be that no one has ever
questioned the high ideals he had for his countrymen.
Perhaps this is why he is greeted with such affection and
deference wherever he goes.

After the brief reign of Sir Alec Douglas-Home, a new

breed of Conservative came to the top. The amateur gentlemen gave way to professionals, technocrats and communicators. Some of the shrewdest members of the old guard turned professional and proved that they could compete on equal terms with the new economic barons. Lord Carrington, a true Renaissance man, is the most outstanding example of the British aristocrat's ability to adapt to changing circumstances.

The new Conservatives came from the ranks of the middle and lower-middle classes. They smelt of after-shave, they wore ready-to-wear suits and shirts and ties made of polyester. They didn't take tea at the Ritz and champagne at the Carlton Club; instead they drank plonk at a wine bar and dined at an Italian bistro. Their status symbols were those of café society: a couple of smart cars in the garage, a villa in the Mediterranean, maybe even a yacht. Socialists too underwent a change. As the Conservative Party declined the Labour Party became fashionable, and upper-middle-class intellectuals flocked to espouse the Labour cause. Britain underwent a mini-cultural revolution; working-class antecedents became the *sine qua non* of social respectability, and inverted snobbery was the rage. Political gurus like Bernard Levin, Paul Johnson and Hugh Thomas vied with each other to pay homage to the founders of the Fabian movement and to exude compassion and social concern through their newspaper columns. On a sartorial level the fashion was to dress down rather than up, and it was commonplace to see people with large bank balances in patched trousers. Formal attire was out and jeans were in. Amongst young people it was difficult to tell the sexes apart as they trailed around in colourful, exotic clothes and long unkempt hair.

Although the new politics of self-reliance have brought

a return of smarter clothes, some Labour intellectuals
still like to manifest a romantic attachment to their
mythical working-class roots through their dress. The
best remembered example was the sight of Michael Foot,
leader of the Labour Party and man of the Hampstead
people, at the annual Remembrance Day ceremony in an
old duffle-coat, when all around were the nation's leaders
in dark suits. It was the working classes, who have strong
views on what is proper, who were the most scandalized
at this lack of respect.

Politics in the post-Macmillan years reflected the
general levelling of society. The governments of Heath,
Wilson and Callaghan left little to choose between them;
all were resolutely middle-middle-class, and their policies were basically pro-Europe, pro-NATO, and pro-
economic expansion at home, just like the social democratic governments in Italy, Germany and Scandinavia
at that time. These other countries had, however, managed to avoid the disruption caused by the nationalization debate, by the increasing but disputed power of the
trade unions, and by conflicts over the value of the
pound, all of which did Britain's public image no good.
Chancellor Schmidt was even reported to have casti-
gated Britain by calling it 'the dustbin of Europe',
although Anglo-German relations were good and, on
more than one occasion, the Germans lent money to
Britain.

In view of Britain's poor image abroad at this time, it
is perhaps not surprising that neither Heath, Wilson nor
Callaghan had much time for foreign correspondents,
despite their claim to be international statesmen. In
Heath's case his dislike was no doubt exacerbated by the
unfortunate press conference when a badly informed
colleague of mine addressed him as 'Mr Grocer'. Heath

was not amused, although everyone else was. It is a sad fact that the British do not seem to realize what influence for good can be exerted by foreign correspondents. Public opinion is moulded by the media, and a willingness to spend a few more minutes explaining the reasons why the British government takes up certain positions on both domestic and international questions would ensure more sympathetic reporting abroad and a greater public understanding of Britain's point of view. Macmillan and Home were well aware of this. Since their time, however, no political leader in Britain has bothered to think further than the domestic media, in marked contrast to their counterparts in other countries. To take but one example, Jacques Chirac, the leader of the French Gaullist Party, employs someone to read and produce a daily digest for him of the English, German and Italian newspapers. Britain appears so far from showing this degree of concern that at the 1983 general election the Conservative Party even sought to exclude foreign correspondents from the daily press briefings, using as an excuse a lack of space. One of Mrs Thatcher's aides was even heard to refer to foreign newspapers as 'foreign funnies'.

In common with other resident foreign correspondents in London in the 1960s and 1970s, I had not much choice other than to chronicle the decline of this once proud nation. The Conservatives lost their identity under Heath, and by 1979 the Labour Party was tearing itself to shreds in destructive ideological debate. For years British workers were paid more than they earned in output, and this illusory economic prosperity accelerated the movement of socialism away from Marxist orthodoxy. Although socialist parties everywhere were mass movements, nowhere on the Continent did they obtain a

continuing period in office. Once they had modified
Marxism so greatly their political appeal was, perhaps,
too vague. They were in danger of becoming merely
alternative parties which would carry out much the same
policies as their opponents. Ideological flexibility became
the rule, and soon even Marxist terminology was called
into question. For Karl Marx it might have seemed as if
the embourgeoisement of the moment, against which he
had fought during his lifetime, was complete. Parliamentary action for social reform remained, however, a social
democratic goal, though disputes arose – in Britain they
were particularly bitter – over how much rationalization
of the means of production was needed to gain the ends
of a more just society. In their ever more passionate
attachment to representative government as opposed to
any form of authoritarianism, whether Christian or lay,
these parties became, in fact, the upholders of the liberal
tradition in the post-war world. They based their view-
point not, as did the Catholic intellectuals, upon the
dictates of divinity and reason, but upon the necessity for
social reform which involved, to an increasing extent, a
pragmatic analysis of society's actual needs. Social
democrats accepted a Marxist analysis of history but
moved away from the ideology of class struggle towards
the ideology of reasonableness. The crisis in the British
Labour Party stemmed from its inability to turn its back
on the rhetoric of class struggle, which to more and more
of its own members as well as to the electorate at large
was increasingly irrelevant and outdated.

By 1976 the British economy was in such a bad way
that the Labour government was forced to go cap in
hand to the International Monetary Fund for a loan to
stop the pound falling. I remember watching Denis
Healey trying to disguise this humiliation by shouting

down his vociferous left-wing opponents at the Labour Party Conference that year with vain protestations that he had no more desire than they to cut public expenditure, as Washington was obliging him to do.

The end of the Callaghan government was a sad affair. This able and popular Prime Minister was undermined by feuding amongst his own supporters, and even his considerable charm was unable to dissipate the growing crisis. The unions took on his government, and the resultant trial of strength nearly brought the country to a halt. When, in the midst of a cold winter made more miserable by uncollected refuse littering the streets, dying people being turned away from hospitals, strike pickets, corpses left unburied and discontent on all sides, the Prime Minister returned from international summitry in the Caribbean and said, 'Crisis? What crisis?', he appalled the electorate with his apparently total loss of grip. After that it was only a matter of time before his government was brought down.

The House of Commons in the last days of the Labour government presented an unedifying spectacle. As the situation in the country deteriorated the frustration of MPs at the lack of effective leadership boiled over in scenes of shouting and high passion. I never thought to see the 'Mother of Parliaments' take on such an Italianate hue – it was a far cry from the 'vastly impressive and moving' proceedings described by Lichtenberg when he visited the House of Commons in 1770. Finally on 28 March 1979 the entire country was gripped by the tension that had seized Parliament, as the first woman to lead a political party in Britain mounted a head-on challenge to the incumbent Prime Minister and won. History was made that day, but not just the personal historical victory of Mrs Thatcher. The British people

had, over the preceding twenty years, become increasingly alienated from the traditional ideology of the
Labour Party and were aching for a return to older
values. They wanted a change in style and substance,
and above all they wanted strong leadership. Mrs
Thatcher promised all these, and the people responded.

Mrs Thatcher was able to offer the British what de
Gaulle had offered the French at the time of the collapse
of the Fourth Republic: a leadership that would satisfy
the nostalgia for a previous era of national greatness.
Mrs Thatcher, like de Gaulle and Winston Churchill, is
a majestic leader. Foreigners understand the sense of
'L'Etat, c'est moi' of the Thatcher reign. The British now
feel confident that their glorious heritage is still existent.
The Empire may have been lost but the Falklands war
clearly demonstrated that, under the right leadership,
the Royal Navy and the British army are as good as they
ever were in the old days and that this country is still
able to defend and to reconquer any of its territory in the
world, no matter how far from the mainland.

Mrs Thatcher's advent signified a turning-point in
British history. She is the defender of the English faith in
the values of authoritarianism and puritanism. Oliver
Cromwell represents the closest historical comparison to
Mrs Thatcher – yet Cromwell is the hero of Tony Benn,
the devoted advocate of British working-class traditions
and interests. All this may explain why Mrs Thatcher
has such a popular appeal. The Prime Minister's
approach and rhetoric reflects the mood of the country,
even if some of her policies are contrary to the interests of
many ordinary people.

— 3 —

Mrs Thatcher gets the top job

' . . . for the British make no distinction as to sex in their rulers' (Tacitus)

On 7 May 1979, Britain led the way into the age of sexual equality when the first woman Prime Minister of a major Western democracy went to kiss the hand of her Queen. Petticoat government was now a reality, and a quiet moan of apprehension was heard to rumble through the bastions of male chauvinism in London's clubland. Changing times had been signalled four years earlier when the officers of the Carlton Club, a temple of Conservatism, had convened a hasty meeting to authorize the upholding of the rule that all leaders of the Conservative Party should be members of the club over the rule that no woman should be a member; and the Tory grandees were obliged to suppress their distress at seeing a woman tripping up and down their Club's magnificent curved staircase, hitherto reserved during the daytime hours for the measured tread of male feet. Mrs Thatcher was pretty, she was smart, she was confident. It was altogether too much that she was also clever.

But clever she was, and far more besides, and the nation soon found out (as Enoch Powell was to put it later) the quality of her mettle. The electorate might have been forgiven for underestimating the strength of her determination because prior to the election of 1979 she had had no major government experience. For all that she had been in Parliament for twenty years and on the front bench for twelve, in the public mind she was mainly thought of with derision as 'Thatcher the milk-snatcher', who had abolished the £8 million a year free milk programme for primary schoolchildren when she was Secretary of State at the Department of Education.

Britain's first woman Prime Minister learnt her politics at her father's knee. Daughter of a small-town grocer, she grew up imbued with the lower-middle-class code of values: self-reliance, hard work, respect for the law, patriotism and economic freedom. 'I've always regarded individualism as a Christian mission,' she is quoted as saying, and her fundamental commitment to democracy and her passionate conviction that all other political systems are a betrayal of the individual are legacies of her father's strongly held and wide-ranging views. It must be emphasized, however, that by individualism she means mainly individual and corporate economic freedom; she has never favoured those aspects of individual freedom that embrace civil liberties, non-conformist lifestyles or liberal moral attitudes.

In most other countries a young person so obviously destined for a political career would begin by taking a degree in law. Margaret Thatcher instead studied science. In this as in so many other ways she demonstrated her willingness to break with accepted norms; female science graduates were thin on the ground in her day, but she saw nothing strange in entering a predominantly male world if it suited her talents. From the earliest age her creed had been the responsibility of the individual to make the most of his or her own potential, to which considerations of sex or class have been entirely irrelevant.

Having got one degree under her belt she allowed herself to be persuaded by a percipient young Tory she had met at Oxford University, Airey Neave, that she should also read for the Bar. Neave had observed her analytical mind at work and had recognized that her intelligence and strong political views would require more public opportunities than were available to the industrial chemist she had become. His early confidence in her continued until his own brutal and untimely death in 1979, four years after he had masterminded her successful campaign for the leadership of the Conservative Party and when she was on the brink of winning the general election of that year.

With the knowledge of law an additional weapon in her armoury, Margaret Thatcher's career followed a pattern familiar to politically committed young people in democracies everywhere, aided by vitally essential good fortune. Equality of opportunity are fine words, but Conservative constituency selection committees are notoriously reluctant to entrust their parliamentary hopes to women. Once again Margaret Roberts, as she then was, showed her determination to compete on equal terms in a man's world. At the age of twenty-three her outstanding qualities overcame the prejudices of the selection committee in Dartford, a Labour-held seat – not that it really mattered, for it was a hopeless seat. Marriage and children occupied the next few years, and then in 1959, aged thirty-two, she won the parliamentary seat of Finchley which she has held ever since. Her abilities quickly brought her to the fore, and within seven years she was on the front bench as shadow spokesman on education.

Here she had her hands full. Students were growing increasingly rebellious, and there was a fierce debate going on in Britain, as elsewhere, over declining standards of education. Tied to this debate was a continuing battle over Labour's desire to reorganize the country's grammar, secondary and technical schools into vast new comprehensive schools that would eschew the academic tracking which many considered an unjust expression of outdated class attitudes. At her first press conference as the opposition's chief spokesman on education in October 1969 Mrs Thatcher took pains to emphasize that she was not an extremist. 'I am not a reactionary,' she insisted. Nevertheless, as a former grammar school girl herself, she had been determined to resist the tide towards what became known as comprehensivization.

When the Tories returned to power under Mr Heath, Mrs Thatcher retained her portfolio and became Secretary of State for Education and Science. At last she was a full member of a British Cabinet. She was not the first woman to serve as Education Minister: that honour had gone to Florence Horsburgh in Winston Churchill's 1951–5 government. But she quickly became by far the best known, although in a highly unflattering way. The outcry over the abolition of free school milk and the continuing unruly state of university campuses led to the *Sun* calling her in 1970 'the most unpopular woman in Britain'.

Overseas such local emotional quarrels did not hold much import. At that time international interest in Britain was centred around the enlargement of the Common Market. After General de Gaulle's historic 'No' to British participation there had been a lot to do to repair the bridges with Europe. The success of new negotiations made the then Prime Minister, Edward

Heath, the most famous Englishman in Europe. Later
on, however, when Britain was plunged into the disaster
of the miners' strike and the three-day week, Heath's
reputation at home and abroad suffered badly. The loss
of two elections in 1974 after a period of humiliating
U-turns and economic chaos sealed his fate. The Conservative Party wanted a change of leader, and above all
someone who would give them a sense of purpose.

It was typical of Mrs Thatcher that on the first ballot
for a new leader she was the only serious candidate
willing to stand up and be counted against Mr Heath –
much to the surprise of many. Sir Keith Joseph disqual-
ified himself after an unfortunate speech at Edgbaston
which attracted much adverse reaction; Edward du
Cann preferred the world of business to the dubious
rewards of high office. Conservative Party leaders, before
Heath, had emerged after discussions behind closed
doors, with any dissension concealed from public view.
Open competition for the top job was still a new and, to
some, distasteful procedure, especially when the incumbent was one of the contenders. It was not until Heath
had been defeated on the first ballot that the party's
heavyweights could bring themselves to throw their hats
into the ring. By then it was too late. The parliamentary
party had already split between the traditionalists and
the militants, and the latter, with Margaret Thatcher as
their champion, were in the ascendant. The entry of
Messrs Whitelaw, Prior, Howe and Peyton into the
contest simply split the traditionalist vote four ways.
Almost without realizing it, the British Conservative
Party, widely regarded abroad as the embodiment of
paternalist reaction and privilege, found itself taking the
most sensational step of any democratic party in Europe
or America: Margaret Thatcher, a girl from the pro-

vinces with unfashionable fire in her belly, was in due course virtually certain to become the Western world's first woman Prime Minister.

Mrs Thatcher's election as leader marked a fundamental turning point in the Conservative Party. The opportunities afforded after the war by vastly improved social services had enabled many more impecunious young people from middle and lower-class backgrounds to enter Parliament. Such people felt little desire to perpetuate the traditional social structure inside the political parties (this applied just as much to bright young graduates on the Labour benches whose way was blocked by time-serving worthies from traditional Labour families or the unions). Having profited by the state system, they also knew their way around its deficiencies. On the Conservative side this led to a growing disillusionment with the psychological fruits of the welfare state – the scrounger mentality, the diversion of brainpower into the challenge of beating the system, and underneath it all the dissipation of will. They were worried too about the effects of post-war Labour governments' large-scale nationalization policies, and felt that any disgruntled group of workers now had the power to cause untold damage, even to bringing down a government, as Heath had learned.

Being a daughter of the people, Mrs Thatcher was closer to them than many of her opponents would admit. (In Parliament, for example, she has always taken great care to keep in touch with her backbenchers, in contrast to Heath's arrogant assumptions of loyalty.) She epitomized British determination to stand up for one's rights, which she saw above all as the individual's right and duty to look after his own economic salvation. Her desire to set private enterprise free was the natural outcome of her youthful experiences in Grantham, with all that she had learnt then about ordinary people's aspirations. It was also the expression of a wave of unease that was sweeping through the country and causing so many young MPs to reject the received wisdom of the last two decades. Times were changing, and Mrs Thatcher was the right person in the right place at the right time to lead a crusade back to a right-wing political ideology.

Overseas commentators showed immense interest in the Thatcher phenomenon as time progressed and the extent of her difference from previous leaders of all British political parties became apparent. Here was a woman who was made for power, whose sole aim was to reverse much of what had been considered enlightened legislation by successive governments over the previous thirty years, and who was thirsting to force back the frontiers of government control of economic activity. In no other European country was such a radical reshaping of the social and economic structure being contemplated, and nowhere else was there such a ferment of intellectual activity taking place in the political arena.

The scientist in Mrs Thatcher was not satisfied with what she considered the unsound basis of many previous Conservative policies. She put the party under the microscope and subjected her findings to a far-reaching programme of analysis and re-evaluation, and everyone with a worthwhile contribution to make participated in the debate. As a result the Conservative Party was an exciting entity to be around during those five years in opposition. Journalists, political commentators, academics, sympathizers and the plain curious came trooping from all corners of the world to test the political climate and stare at this amazing woman. The party's international office dealt with a constant stream of foreign dignitaries and commentators eager to shake her hand (236 from 46 countries in 1979) while the London correspondents of overseas news media were badgered relentlessly by their editors for interviews with La Thatcher. Most were left to observe from afar, however, as Mrs Thatcher was far too busy conducting a domestic revolution to concern herself with foreigners who had no votes.

While in opposition Mrs Thatcher's lack of concern with foreign affairs was a weak spot in her overall political makeup. It was unlucky that her shadow Foreign Secretary, John Davies, died, thus leaving the main burden of formulating foreign policy to the deputy foreign affairs spokesmen, Douglas Hurd and Richard Luce. As a former member of the Foreign Office, Douglas Hurd was particularly sensitive to the need for Mrs Thatcher to project herself, her policies and her philosophy beyond the shores of Great Britain, but neither he nor anyone else succeeded in persuading her to capitalize on the enormous reservoir of goodwill abroad. As a result, much potentially favourable overseas press coverage of the Conservative Party in opposition went unwritten. However, centre-right parties in other countries were stimulated by Mrs Thatcher's restatement of Conservative principles, and it was during this period that the final negotiations took place leading to the setting up in 1978 of the European Democratic Union, a centre-right answer to the Socialist International. The increased co-operation across frontiers which arose from the EDU was demonstrated five years later when the Norwegian Conservative Prime Minister was the first foreign politician to state his total support for Mrs

Thatcher following the Argentinian invasion of the Falkland Islands.

Frustrating as Europeans found Mrs Thatcher's lack of interest in them, it is a truism that there is little electoral mileage anywhere in foreign affairs, particularly for an opposition party. She was right therefore to concentrate on domestic matters. Her priorities were the traditional Tory ones of cutting public expenditure and placing emphasis on the maintenance of law and a credible defence policy. The crucial difference between her approach and Ted Heath's was that she was above all seeking to achieve these within the context of a clearly defined Conservative philosophy. She considered that Mr Heath had latterly handed the propaganda victory to socialism, and it was not surprising that his administration had been blown around like a rudderless ship in the grip of an adverse gale. Chief among the influences to shape her thinking was Sir Keith Joseph, who set up the Centre for Policy Studies as a think-tank of the new right and an addendum to the Conservative Research Department, which in her view was tainted with Heathite, left-wing Toryism. Sir Keith's lieutenant at the CPS, Alfred Sherman (now Sir Alfred), was a former Communist who had fought in the Spanish Civil War, typical of other left-wing intellectuals who underwent a Pauline conversion to become ardent participants in the development of a Thatcherite philosophy.

Notwithstanding the considerable input of right-wing thinking from the CPS and the Institute of Economic Affairs, as well as from academics and specialists of all sorts, Mrs Thatcher kept many of Mr Heath's close associates in her shadow Cabinet. Their effect was to temper her own philosophies so that the policies which were developed in opposition were acceptable to a

broader range of Conservative opinion than might other-
wise have been the case. Thus the divergence between
Mrs Thatcher's bellicose rhetoric and her more cautious
actions became apparent early on, as she sought to
project herself to the electorate while retaining maximum
support inside the parliamentary party.

The public image of Mrs Thatcher as a forceful
champion of the individual was reinforced by national
political events during her years as leader of the opposition when the 1974–9 Labour government was beset with
mounting problems as the recession set in. Neither
Harold Wilson nor James Callaghan was able to get a
grip on increasing unemployment or labour unrest. The
former was despised for the transparent trickery he had
used to keep his party together, and the latter became
increasingly out of touch with the ordinary voter. Only
one political leader was willing to take on the unions
after the strikes of the Winter of Discontent: Margaret
Thatcher.

When the Labour government fell in March 1979, Mrs
Thatcher swung into the election campaign with enormous enthusiasm, convinced that she, and not the
Labour Party, was now the voice of the people. I
watched her talking to stall-holders and shoppers in East
End markets, comparing the prices of oranges and
tomatoes, echoing ordinary peoples' worries about the
accelerating increase in prices. Hers was a real dialogue,
as one housewife to another, and when she promised to
give priority to the battle against inflation people listened
to her. The government of the country had been visibly
sliding into impotence, and the people responded to a
politician who manifestly knew what she believed to be
right and was conspicuously eager and strong enough to
lead from the front.

Mrs Thatcher's phenomenal energy and stamina astounded all observers throughout the election campaign. Here was a woman who was driven by fury at the damage being done to her country by vested working-class interests, by scorn at the weakness of her compatriots' moral fibre, by indignation at the inefficiencies perpetrated by an inflexible bureaucracy. Within days her blazing determination to restore self-respect and responsibility to the British people had captured the moral high ground of the political landscape, and her campaign became a crusade. Jim Callaghan in his 'bovine splendour' (as the *Spectator* described him) looked like a beached whale; his native element had rejected him and suddenly hurricanes were shrieking over his stranded bulk. His fireside chat mode of talking comfortably to the people lost all credibility, and as the weeks passed he looked increasingly irrelevant. The Labour Party destroyed its own chances by its fractiousness in the face of a Conservative Party inspired by a charismatic leader, herself certain of triumph. It may have been a former Labour Prime Minister, Harold Wilson, who talked of the need for a revival of the Dunkirk spirit, but it was a Tory leader and a woman whose courage and indomitable determination carried the nation with her on a route march to victory over apathy, pusillanimity and sloth.

The whole world took a tremendous interest in the British general election of 1979. Westminster was swarming with foreign journalists and TV and radio crews all intent on outwitting harassed press officers at the party headquarters when they could not get what they wanted by direct means. This election broke new ground on several counts: not only was the potential Prime Minister a woman, but never before had the role of an advertising agency (Saatchi and Saatchi were the chosen company) been so conspicuous, with an aggressive, imaginative and manipulative campaign – for the first time the great British viewing public did not with one accord go and make the tea when the Conservative Party political broadcasts came on the screen. But Mrs Thatcher never allowed the high-pressure sales techniques, the gimmickry or the media circus to come between her and the people, nor did she admit to her own unique status as the probable first woman Prime Minister of a major Western democracy. Several unwary visiting journalists who tried to follow that tack found themselves roundly ticked off for daring to suggest that her sex could have any bearing on her ability to fulfil the highest role in the government.

No 'ifs' and 'buts' weakened her dialogue with the electorate; her style was, as it remains, direct, and her speeches easily understandable by all strata of society; and as the voters were gradually swept up in the current of her enthusiasm, so she seemed to establish an intensely personal relationship with the mass of ordinary men and women, as if she had discovered a source of mystic refreshment deep in the national psyche which only needed to be tapped for Britain's ancient glories to revive again. Hardened observers of politics the world over were confounded by Mrs Thatcher's absolute faith in her own rightness, and by the people's willingness to trust this latter-day Boadicea.

On election night itself, Smith Square, in the heart of Westminster (where both the Labour and Conservative Party headquarters were then situated), became a theatre. All day long TV technicians had been installing powerful lights on the steps of St John's, in the centre of the square, illuminating both parties' front entrances,

and as the evening came on so the elder Tory statesmen
began to gather at the Conservative Party's home at No.
32 in anticipation of what seemed certain to be a
Conservative victory. Soon after the ballot boxes closed
at ten o'clock, a crowd collected on the pavement outside
No. 32. At two o'clock in the morning Mrs Thatcher
arrived from her north London constituency to be
greeted by a great roar in the quiet night air as the crowd
saluted their conquering heroine. The contrast with the
pavement outside the Labour Party's headquarters,
Transport House, fifty yards away, was almost poignant:
there was only darkness and inactivity, only two or three
policemen to control a handful of supporters, while
across the square rows of grinning bobbies were assuring
the next Prime Minister safe passage through her ador-
ing fans. Elsewhere in London champagne flowed like
water wherever two or three Conservatives were
gathered together, and in Trafalgar Square revellers
celebrated in traditional fashion by jumping into the
fountains. This joyful outburst of high spirits was remarkable in this era of electoral apathy.

Was Mrs Thatcher inevitable? When she came in,
pledged against an incomes policy and promising a
society in which the background of a non-depreciating
currency would make self-discipline possible, she was
acting on the logic of history. The spendthrift course of
the old sort of social democracy had reduced itself to
absurdity. Change was inevitable, either towards state
socialism or towards an economically freer yet morally
more austere society, and the direction it took was
determined by the Tories' rather improbable choice of
this woman, at precisely the moment when the mood of
the country was in tune with her political philosophy and
personal style. In a democracy, which provides no scope

for Norman conquests and dynastic politics, sailing the tide of inevitability to reach a chosen destination is the better part of leadership.

— 4 —

Shooting wars – The Iron Lady takes on Galtieri and Scargill

It is not given to many British Prime Ministers to fight a shooting war. Those who do, and win, can be certain that the patriotic public will accord them their due measure of glory. Mrs Thatcher is thus assured of her place in the history books.

It was both Britain's and Mrs Thatcher's good fortune that the Falkland Islands dispute should flare up into hostilities when she, temperamentally a war leader *par excellence*, was at No. 10. With the exception of Winston Churchill, which other Prime Minister this century would have reacted so decisively to the Argentinian invasion of the Falklands? Even Anthony Eden, willing as he was to use force in defence of Britain's economic interests at Suez, would probably not have rushed for the guns quite so fast on behalf of an under-populated and economically valueless patch of British territory just across the sea from the South Pole. But Mrs Thatcher comes from that strain of Englishmen and women for whom compromise in the face of an unwarranted provocation is out of the question. When the challenger is one of the despised Latin races, and a comic-opera South American one at that, no true blue Brit is going to let him get away with it unpunished. Slow to anger but unshakeably determined, the bulldog breed sets out with single-minded patriotism to avenge the insult to its pride.

Mrs Thatcher was the right woman for the hour. With her unerring instinct for popular feeling, she knew that the British people would expect her to retaliate fittingly to the gauntlet thrown down by the Argentinians. No matter how much intellectuals and 'opinion-formers' might pussyfoot around, the man on the Clapham omnibus looked to her to take decisive action – and she did. When diplomacy all too obviously failed, she called the First Sea Lord and ordered the Royal Navy to sail to reconquer the islands. The speed of reaction, the weight of arms (and support) that was mobilized, the clarity and courage with which the issues were set out, were her responsibility and hers alone.

For a few days the world held its breath, amazed. Was a democracy really going to fight for its own people? Was the whole unwieldy edifice which the West had set up over the last forty years to avoid decision, to fudge issues, to counter aggression with sanctions and resolutions and hot air in profusion, going to be by-passed? Above all, world opinion asked itself with a mixture of envy and admiration, were the British really no different from what they had been in 1940?

Not the least of Mrs Thatcher's achievements was the speed with which she mustered international support. Naturally enough the Commonwealth countries were right behind her, and so was a majority of the United Nations Security Council when it passed Resolution 502 condemning the invasion as soon as it had happened. In Europe President Mitterrand sent a personal message of support, while all other Western European governments (except Spain, not surprisingly) and the Community of Ten expressed varying degrees of outrage. Such prompt reactions were not merely a show of democratic solidarity in the face of unjustifiable aggression, they were even more a tribute to Mrs Thatcher's determination to resist this insult to her territory and her people. Economic sanctions were imposed by the Europeans against Argentina, only to be lifted first by Italy and then by the other Community countries when it seemed clear that the invaders would be defeated. The Americans, after a suitable period of hesitation due to their split loyalties between old allies and important neighbours, seemed relieved when Argentinian obduracy enabled them to throw their weight behind Mrs Thatcher. And even on the South American continent several countries made clear their dislike of their big neighbour's arrogance. By the time the troops went into battle Mrs Thatcher had the comfort of knowing they had world opinion on their side.

Back home this was not uniformly the case, however. The overwhelming majority of Members of Parliament remained, to their personal credit, dedicated to the principle that no settlement should leave the Argentinian aggressor better placed than before the invasion force arrived. But the churches, the media, the City and the establishment had long been conditioned to the received wisdom that might is wrong and that negotiation is to be preferred to military confrontation in all circumstances. They found it distasteful to admit that public opinion, both in Britain and abroad, had overtaken them and that the diplomatic option was no longer feasible. Along with the rest of the world they watched in amazement as the Royal Navy (which they had been told was a shadow of its former self) was assembled, armed and despatched by a post-imperial kingdom (which they had been told was bankrupt and divided) to the very farthest corner of the globe to 'save' some 1,800 of its citizens.

The very fact that the Falklanders were so few in number was what made the decision to rescue them by force truly heroic, in the classical and Pyrrhic sense. The whole world now watched film of these people on their TV screens and saw that they were ordinary, peaceful folk – not spies or government officials, like the American hostages in Teheran, nor golf-club majors, like the settlers in Rhodesia. The clusters of neat pink-washed houses, indistinguishable from any harbour village on the west coast of Scotland, had the lowest crime rate of any community in the southern hemisphere, and the Falkland Islanders sought only to live in peace, unglamorous and hard-working, out of the headlines and remote from everything unconnected with sheep. Even the world-weary sophisticates back home eventually rationalized their reluctant support for the war by a romantic sympathy with the islanders' wish to be left alone.

The cost of this expedition was immense, and put the government itself at risk. If anything had gone wrong, if the *Hermes* or the *Invincible* had been sunk, the government might have fallen. Mrs Thatcher put her political career on the line in order to uphold the principle that the Falklands should remain British; ironically, it has been calculated that for the money spent on the war, each and every Falklander could have been resettled elsewhere and given over £1 million to start a new life.

For Margaret Thatcher there was no doubt about the outcome of the war: Britain was certain to succeed. However,it was later realized that proverbial British luck had played an important role in Mrs Thatcher's favour. Her victory at the other end of the world was also a victory at home. Alone she showed the world, as Winston

Churchill had done in 1940, that the British will not be pushed around and that they will defend their national pride whenever it lies in their power to do so. By her leadership she restored the British people's sense of nationalism and their faith in the rightness of military solutions; whatever opinions people may hold of her domestic performance, no one denies her courage or the electrifying effect she had on national morale.

As if one confrontation with violence was not enough, her personal heroism was called upon a second time two years later when an IRA bomb came close to killing the entire British Cabinet during the Conservative Party Conference in Brighton. The world watched horror-struck as dazed ministers were dug out of the rubble of the Grand Hotel. Even more striking to foreign eyes was Mrs Thatcher's determination when she insisted that the final sessions of the Party Conference, including her speech, should take place the next day as planned. In any other country such a conference would have broken up in confusion – not in Britain. Margaret Thatcher, shocked and shaken at the death and suffering of her friends, stood in the conference centre next door to the ruined Grand Hotel to show the IRA and the world that she was alive and more determined than ever to pursue business as usual.

IRA operations mounted in Britain have traditionally had two objectives. One is the long-term task of sickening British public opinion so that pressures will mount for withdrawal from Ireland, while the other, just as important; is to have an effect on morale in Ireland itself and, crucially, on the fund-raising elements in the USA.

In the immediate aftermath of the bomb, Conservative politicians were insistent that the government would not be deflected by the activities of the IRA from seeking political progress in Northern Ireland, but as a result of the attempted massacre at Brighton Mrs Thatcher appeared to be unable to make any moves that would involve Dublin because these might be interpreted as concessions made under pressure from the IRA. The Prime Minister, when interviewed a few weeks later, was less than encouraging about her hopes for any future initiative. The Dublin proposals for a so-called forum to involve the Republic in the running of Ulster were rejected. The revolutionary strategy of the IRA and its political arm, Sinn Fein, may have been successful in stopping a permanent agreement between London and Dublin.

There are no such doubts about Mrs Thatcher's handling of the miners' strike. Once again the international media took a close interest in a British domestic crisis. This time, although the Prime Minister's personal role was initially almost invisible to the public, no one doubted that it was her determination above all that eventually broke Arthur Scargill. When Mr Heath had tried to fight the miners they had defeated him, for he failed to get his message across convincingly to the electorate whereas the miners caught the public's sympathy with their image of honest, cheery, hard-working men on whose backs the nation's economic wealth almost literally rested. The Labour Party and the other unions gave this first miners' strike for half a century their full support, and to Mr Heath's question 'Who rules the country?' the people replied that he certainly did not.

Mrs Thatcher took the lesson to heart. Despite her rhetoric she was in fact prepared to appease the miners herself when there was unrest in the pits during her first term of office. However, she knew as everyone else did that National Union of Mineworkers president Arthur Scargill was motivated by the desire for a political confrontation with her when he called a miners' strike soon after her re-election. Mr Scargill remained true to his convictions by seeking to overthrow the government by extra-parliamentary means, but he was eventually defeated by the irreconcilable divisions among the miners themselves. As the months wore on Mr Scargill attracted enormous hostility from the media and deep mistrust for his disregard for democratic rights and ambivalence towards violence. Even so, he retained sufficient support throughout the strike to have brought down a lesser person than Mrs Thatcher. At the beginning of the dispute she avoided being drawn into direct confrontation with the miners' president, but she made sure that her own interpretation of the strike was made crystal clear to the public through statements in Parliament. At the outset she had followed the advice of Energy Secretary Peter Walker, who had insisted that the miners' dispute was with their employers, the National Coal Board, and not with the government. As time dragged on, however, she became increasingly concerned that the propaganda battle was going Scargill's way, especially when the Board developed a lamentable tendency to shoot itself in the foot with well-publicized internal disagreements about the handling of the strike. She was even more worried about the loss of revenue and the huge cost of policing the strike. In the end she lost patience with the inconclusive and increasingly bitter way things were going, and in an interview with Sir Alastair Burnet she made it clear that she personally was going to take the decisions from then on. Scargill had to be defeated 'pour décourager les autres', to prevent disputes of this kind.

She was unwittingly aided in her firm stand by the National Union of Mineworkers' total failure to obtain backing for the strike from any other unions. As the miners themselves were increasingly violently divided on the issue, it was useless to expect any other union leader to bring his members out on their behalf. The terrible threat of action by the traditional 'triple alliance' of coal, steel and rail vanished into thin air when the steelworkers said 'No thanks' and only a handful of railwaymen said 'Well, maybe'. Then the power station workers refused to have anything to do with such blatantly unproductive goings-on. Without the support of these workers no other union could make much impact, and the union movement as a whole clearly had no stomach for the fight. It was said that at the height of the dispute Arthur Scargill went to TUC headquarters and accosted the members of the Executive Committee as they left their meeting with the question: 'Well, Comrades, when is the general strike going to be?' to which they replied: 'You missed it, Comrade, it was in 1926.'

In Parliament the Prime Minister had little to fear from the opposition benches. Tony Benn spent more time making speeches at miners' rallies than in the House (126 as against 10). Neil Kinnock did not attempt to hide his distaste for the strike, and what could have been dangerous for a newly elected and very inexperienced leader of the Labour Party in fact proved the reverse. He was already in tune with public opinion, which was not about to give the miners much sympathy just ten years after the generous settlement they had won for themselves by paralyzing the country in the depths of the 1974 winter – it was common knowledge that the miners' standard of living, what with mortgages, expensive cars and holidays abroad, was sufficiently middle-class to lose them all credibility when they cried poverty, and in 1984 too many other people were unemployed (or a lot worse off than the miners) for the public to spare any sympathy for what was widely seen as an arbitrary, unjustified and wholly political campaign.

Foreign observers found the course of the miners' strike fascinating to watch. Several other countries, particularly in Europe, had after all been facing similar crises in their coal industries with just as much deleterious effect on mining communities. Yet they had come through them with far less bitterness and destruction.

And the end of it all? A whimper, not a bang. And perhaps that best illustrates the extent of Mrs Thatcher's achievement in the major crises she has had to face. Through her determined leadership she has given her people confidence to emulate her in tackling their problems themselves. Her trade union legislation has made it possible for non-militant union members to have more control over what their unions do in their names; her determination to uphold law and order and to confront aggressors and terrorists has inspired a new mood of self-reliance and refusal to be bullied. Above all she can be credited with making the island race once more very proud of its 'Englishness'. Some of her adversaries talk about 'jingoism' and one can see by reading some of the headlines in the British press that some of the best-known clichés about 'the other side of the Channel' have been re-used to create a new climate of fanatical nationalism. Some foreigners appear to be hurt by this attitude, but in the main the British have good reason to be optimistic. Their country has never been so respected since the end of the war, though, for Mrs Thatcher, the main target remains the success of her economic policies.

In Britain bread and butter have a longer-lasting

electoral impact than guns and victories. Inflation is down but unemployment is too high and so is the interest rate. The battle of the statistics may go on for ever and the government may put forward some convincing arguments to persuade the public of its successes, but its economic policies may take years before they come to fruition and . . . the election is not too far away.

— 5 —

The opposition from the left, the right and the centre

A government as radical as Mrs Thatcher's will inevitably attract more opposition than the consensus governments which have ruled Britain since the Second World War. There are no half-measures with Mrs Thatcher; for everyone who admires her and thinks she is on the right track, someone else anathematizes her as the destructive genius of Britain's industrial and social infrastructure.

The Labour Party is of course her most vociferous enemy. The combination of her policies and her style is a gift to the demagogues of the left, who seem to get an almost cathartic pleasure from whipping themselves into frenzies of denunciation. The scale of the Tory landslides in 1979 and 1983 and the bitter splits within the Labour Party have led some Conservatives to write Labour off as a spent force, doomed to disappear in the manner of the Liberals after Lloyd George.

But no one knows better than Mrs Thatcher that much of the British electorate invariably votes as their forefathers did (the bedrock vote), and not for one moment has she underestimated the danger from Labour's heartland. The one constant in the next election is that Labour, even with the polytechnic lecturers

77

at the gates, has an irreducible strength of around 220
seats and a kind of sullen immortality. Labour could
afford the luxury of internecine warfare when it departed
into a minimum of four years' opposition. The perpetual-
ly competing forces of democratic evolution and revolution, which have characterized the socialist movement in
Britain since its earliest roots in Liberal and Marxist
philosophy, and which 'Sunny' Jim Callaghan had
allowed to flourish under his opportunist rule, were
embarked on another round in their struggle for domi-
nance of the party.

Under the romantic but ineffectual leadership of
Michael Foot – who, like the Bourbons, had learnt
nothing and forgotten nothing – the party was divided;
electors had lost faith in the ability of the moderate
mainstream to control the extreme left and were desert-
ing the party in droves. Socialism in the post-Falklands
climate seemed an aberration from traditional British
bloody-minded independence, and the voters appeared
to want none of it. And the Conservatives' one sure
winner of a policy, the sale of council homes, had
convinced many former Labour voters that it was the
Conservative Party after all that best understood their
aspirations.

By 1983 Michael Foot was on his way out, the party
fragmented, and traditional Labour supporters despair-
ing. The trumpet of Bennery was heard loud in the land.
But once again, as so many times before, Labour opted
for compromise in the post-general election leadership
contest. The standard of socialism passed to a young
Welshman, untried in government, short on political
acumen, inexperienced and unknown, his only qualifica-
tion seeming to be that no one could agree on anyone
else. Neil Kinnock's early performances at Prime Minis-

ter's question time in the House of Commons were embarrassingly inept, and the Prime Minister had no difficulty in demolishing his long-winded Welsh oratory with a few clear-cut English slogans. For a while it seemed as if the fresh-faced innocent would never match up to the skill of an old pro.

But then things started to change. Traditional British sympathy for the underdog rallied moderates to his side. Many people preferred to suspend judgement until he had been given time to get a grip on the horrendous problems facing the Labour Party. Denis Healey was not alone in asserting that Neil Kinnock would grow into the job. Two years after his election, Kinnock is vindicating that faith. Paradoxically he has been helped by those very circumstances that at first threatened to destroy him. The power of the left and its thirst for martyrdom, the driving ambition of demagogues claiming a mandate from 'the masses' in their chosen cause, the emphasis on ideological purity over pragmatic politics, the intolerance, self-satisfaction and humourlessness of many militant activists (with the notable exception of Ken Livingstone) – all these factors combined to make the average Labour voter think that Neil Kinnock was all that stood between him and a thoroughly undesirable enforced egalitarianism.

The contrast between Kinnock and Benn, Meacher, Scargill, and so on was paralleled on the right by the adversarial relations that Mrs Thatcher delights in. Kinnock may not yet be a match for her in Parliament, but he has got her licked on television. She can be tense, dictatorial, inflexible. He is affable, relaxed, and notably temperate in his promises and general outlook. Is he planning to inject £15 billion, £20 billion, £25 billion into the economy? Good God, no! Something of the order of

£5 billion or £4 billion, possibly £2 billion or conceivably even less, might meet the case. So Neil worries about inflation? Indeed he does. Inflation is a very serious matter and there is going to be none of it under Labour. Everything must be done in a calm and ordered way. Bags of co-operation is the name of the game. The lion will lie down with the lamb, and capitalists will bless the day Labour came to power as they count up their extra millions.

Kinnock's growing self-assurance is having its effect right across the political left. He undeniably commands the support of a majority of Labour voters, both within Parliament and outside it, and is now credible as an alternative Prime Minister. Those far-left militants who are ambitious for government are now openly abseiling across the face of British politics, away from their former gurus or companions-in-arms towards the safer prospects of a middle way; Meacher is distancing himself from Benn, Livingstone has forsaken Knight, and everyone has ditched Scargill. Kinnock's bandwagon is now the one on which everyone wants to jump. And Kinnock is more fortunate than Mrs Thatcher in the support he gets from his party's elder statesmen. Wilson and Callaghan's general approval of him is worth more in the ratings than Mr Heath's angry opposition to Mrs Thatcher. And while the likes of Francis Pym, Jim Prior and Ian Gilmour rumble warningly from the Tory back benches, one of the finest minds in British politics, that of Denis Healey, is firmly deployed in support of his youthful leader. Labour's front bench, in fact, is looking increasingly like an alternative government. The phenomenally energetic Roy Hattersley is nobody's fool, and there are plenty of clever rising stars, such as John Smith, George Foulkes and Gerald Kaufman.

The rehabilitation of Labour is robbing the Alliance of much of its *raison d'être*. The Liberals pose no threat to anyone under the present electoral system, though the historically minded British quite enjoy having this 'alternative' party leavening the lump of main-stream politics. The SDP on the other hand takes itself far more seriously. This fruit of the schisms in the Labour Party has considerable destructive potential for both Labour and the Conservatives; the surprise is only that it has failed to keep up its initial momentum. By now it should be challenging Labour and taking Labour seats, but instead it is pulling in disaffected Tories who have no stomach for the rivers of blood, sweat and tears resulting from Mrs Thatcher's policies.

In Parliament, however, the SDP seem to have made very little impression. With the single exception of Dr Owen, who could have wandered in from a boulevard play, all profile and brass neck, they are invisible and inaudible. They started as they meant to go on, a slick, chic operation aimed exclusively at the media – no vulgar mass rallies were needed to launch this 1980s-style party, distinguished by its brains, its moderation, above all its good taste. The media were invited to breakfast at the Connaught Rooms. Sadly, many of the foreign journalists confused the rather tatty Connaught Rooms with The Connaught, one of the best hotels in London. Their expenses gained: their stories did not. The best account of the event is given by Edward Pearce in his *Senate of Lilliput*, the book no MP dares to read:

The Four (Shirley Williams, Roy Jenkins, William Rodgers and David Owen) sat on a raised dais, the eleven defecting members (more were to follow) sat on a lower dais. Questions were put by the press. The Four spoke,

the eleven kept dutifully silent. Plastic folders containing
publicity material were distributed. We were told that
the mould would be broken, that people were tired of the
old adversarial politics, and, quite reasonably, that
detailed SDP policies would have to wait for development. On the strength of proposals made since – twelve
regional prime ministers and all – absence of policy was
the least of their problems. But give or take the odd
Tammany Irish member, they are a respectable party.
Their MPs are clones of the quiet-and-well-behaved-
young-man-hoping-to-be-made-a-junior-minister.
Messrs Wrigglesworth, Cartwright, Maclennan – all are
washed, correctly dressed, well-spoken, sons any mother
would be proud to have, and with about a quarter of an
ounce of personality between them. But this if anything
enhances them with the public.

At that time the Gang of Four dominated politics. Many
American and European observers predicted that Shirley
Williams would take Margaret Thatcher's place in
Downing Street – Iron Lady out, Velvet Lady in. But
Shirley is still waiting for the bus to Westminster, the
Gang of Four has become the Gang of David. At one
time the Tories called the SDP 'Labour Party, Mark
Two', but now such Tory stalwarts as *The Spectator*'s Jock
Bruce-Gardyne hail David Owen as the successor to the
Iron Lady. Owen's Alliance partner, David Steel, by
contrast, is involved in endless disputes with the more
militant Young Liberals. Even so, the Liberals still have
a much stronger local electoral base than the SDP and
will always be able to maintain certain seats. At the
moment the Alliance can certainly hope to hold the
balance after the next General Election. But a hung
Parliament will put serious strains on the Alliance, for
many Liberals would prefer an association with Labour,
regarded by the SDP as 'the Loony Left'.

The most interesting phenomenon of the Thatcher years is the split that has occurred in the Conservative Party. Tories like to say that their party is a broad church, tolerant of many varying viewpoints, but since 1975 a purified-by-fire orthodoxy has taken over with no room for deviationists. Those who disagree with the central tenets of the faith are 'not one of us' and are banished from the presence of She-who-must-be-obeyed. The brutality of the Thatcher treatment left dissenters reeling in the early days of her reign, so that it was a while before they could collect themselves enough to fight back. Some opted out. A clutch of the gentler sort of Young Conservatives declared themselves for the SDP, and for a while it was rumoured that some disaffected MPs would follow them. In the end the SDP had to make do with just one, Christopher Brocklebank-Fowler. Opposition to Mrs Thatcher is certainly widespread on the left of the party, but it is resigned. No man is willing to risk his political or any other virility by staging a coup which would be bound to fail at this time. Rather the Wets will wait for her to overreach herself and implode, at which point they will step in to rescue the party from its Boadicea-like adventure. Meanwhile they have no choice but to remain at a distance, discoursing in a gentlemanly fashion and lamenting the crude inclination of the British voter to support uncivilized nineteenth-century policies.

To begin with Mrs Thatcher surrounded herself with Wets, who naturally enough had the longest track record at the top of the party. But as she grew more confident, finely-tuned as she is to the pulse of the electorate, she was less willing to tolerate half-hearted support or downright obstructionism, especially in the face of Heath's bitterly self-righteous denunciation of her policies. Christopher Patten was the first brave man to stand up publicly and fight for his point of view when he was secretary to the shadow Cabinet, for which he was banished from that position and from his job as director of the Conservative Research Department. The citizens of Bath adopted him as their own, however, and elected him in 1979 to confront her from behind. He is now back in the ministerial ranks, as Mrs Thatcher has realized that one of the finest minds in the party would be better employed in a difficult job than in pointing out her own defects to the public. Sir Ian Gilmour was next, followed later by Francis Pym and Jim Prior. All three were gentleman farmers of the old school, patrician representatives of responsible Toryism. The trouble was that they saw themselves as responsible for the well-being of their own and all other workers. Mrs Thatcher on the contrary thought that if people would only pull themselves together and stop whingeing there would be no reason for anyone to be responsible for his neighbour at all.

Perhaps this morality of self-sufficiency is the reason for the continued presence in Mrs Thatcher's Cabinet of Peter Walker, the one remaining declared Wet at the top of the party. The grocer's daughter from Grantham and the grocer's son from suburban London share a common background, after all, which is not that of the landed gentry. Mr Walker's ability to adapt and survive is not universally admired, however. Some see him as the inside contender for the leader's diadem when the time comes, while others consider him superficial with all the constancy of a chameleon. His admirers, particularly the young Turks of the Tory Reform Group, regard him as their guru, and his book, *The Ascent of Britain*, is their political bible. The radical views he expressed there on race and inner cities have left some socialists with an inferiority complex; Eric Heffer even gave it a rave review in *Labour Weekly*.

Walker's 'loyal opposition' to the reign of Queen Maggie over the Conservative Party may be the loudest, but it is certainly not the most remarkable. The former Prime Minister, Mr Heath, felt that the Iron Lady snatched his leadership of the Conservative Party and that she is not prepared to recognize him or his merits. In 1975 the late Airey Neave returned to his room from the champagne party in celebration of Mrs Thatcher's victory to notice that the old guard of the Tory Party was not in a mood for rejoicing. One of the leading Wets, sacked by the Iron Lady, told the *Spectator*, 'At the first Shadow Cabinet meeting there was a desperate feeling that the Conservative Party had met a calamitous fate.' The Heath supporters were frustrated from the beginning. It is no mystery that neither James Prior, Francis Pym, Lord Soames nor Sir Ian Gilmour had ever been happy about the new leader's policies or her style of government (or shadow government), nor were a number of backbenchers who were nostalgic for the relaxing days when the Conservative Party did not differ too much from the moderate Labour Party of Hugh Gaitskell.

But only in May 1985 has a proper opposition group been formed – a little party inside the party. It has been said that the 'Centre Forward Group' founded by Mr Francis Pym, together with twenty-nine other Tory MPs, is a sort of spring group like the Tory Reform Group, the Monday Club, or the Bow Group, created to discuss and support new policies for the Tory Party. The Centre Forward Group could have been the Conservative equivalent to the Labour Tribune Group, committed to pursue left-wing Tory policies, but Francis Pym, in launching his initiative, has made it clear that the new group has an anti-Thatcher faction committed enough to be prepared to vote with Labour in the House of Commons against her policies. The Tory paper, the *Sun*, has commented:

> Mock Tories – Francis Pym and his band of Wet Willies have come out of the woodwork to challenge Mrs Thatcher. They claim they are only attacking Tory policies and not the leader. Piffle. They know full well Margaret Thatcher and her policies are indivisible. Of course they are attacking her leadership and if they had the guts they would say so openly. And as the saying has it: Put up. Or Shut Up.

Outside Parliament opposition to Mrs Thatcher is widespread, which is of course what a radical Prime Minister would expect – if she heard no howls of protest she would think her crusade had failed. The revolutionary element in current British politics, however, is the extent to which the rank and file of all sorts of special interest groups do not agree with their leaders' headlong rush for confrontation. They may not vote Conservative (although many of them do, especially their wives), but they are damned if they are going to let themselves be used as riot-fodder for someone else's ego trip. If Mrs Thatcher has done one thing, she has restored to ordinary people the possibility of doing what *they* think is right. The British have always been willing to make a stand on principle, and the failure of the miners' strike is a classic example of the individual's refusal to be bullied. This is why the fire and thunder of Arthur Scargill, Tony Benn, Ray Buckton and others of that ilk hold no terror for Mrs Thatcher. On the contrary, the Tories love them; each one carries a solid 24-carat guarantee to frighten the living daylights out of the electors and secure the return of Tory governments well into the future. Ken Livingstone they love rather less. From being 'Red Ken', the vilified bogeyman of the populist right-wing media, his good humour, quiet reasonableness and evident humanity have won the grudging respect of the man in the street and even the man in the TV studio, to such an extent that Mrs Thatcher is being obliged to disenfranchise Londoners to get rid of him.

Since Arthur Scargill became president of the National Union of Mineworkers, the coal-mining industry has been in turmoil. There have been two national ballots on strike action, which the membership rejected. Finally it was stampeded into an overtime ban, and then a strike which closed three-quarters of the industry for more than a year. The ban cut miners' earnings drastically, and the strike reduced them to virtually nothing. Customers made alternative arrangements to free themselves from dependence on coal. Miner was set against miner, and their families too. Small traders in mining communities went bust on a wide scale. Despite his fire-eating rhetoric, his followers failed to follow him to the end, and his grand design has petered out with barely a whimper.

Tony Benn has not been an overall asset to the Labour Party. Despite losing the deputy leadership contest by a hair's breadth to Denis Healey in 1981, Mr Benn has assiduously worked his way into a position where he has made sure that Conference will see his policies implemented. MPs are now subject to reselection, so that they are constantly under threat from constituency party zealots if they deviate from the party line, and Labour's leader is henceforth to be chosen by Conference and not, as before, by the MPs. And the result? At the last election

Labour gained a smaller percentage of votes than at any time since 1918. All the Tories need to do is show pictures of the Labour Conference in full cry to garner the votes of the silent majority.

All in all, Mrs Thatcher could be thought to be pretty safe for a while yet. Of course politicians on all sides, including her own, are working towards unseating her, pressure groups will continue to cry fury in the streets, vested interests will protest and plot in defence of their own, bishops will dissent and academics will be as ungracious as only academics know how. But Mrs Thatcher relishes a good scrap and will see them all off, one after another, if necessary without any help from her friends.

— 6 —

Britain and Thatcher
– the magic formula

Margaret Thatcher is seen by those on the other side of the Channel as the personification of Britain in the 1980s. Both Mrs Thatcher and her country appear to the 'natives' south of Calais as arrogant, self-opinionated, middle-class throwbacks to the Victorian era.

The French magazine *Nouvel Observateur* recently printed a report on Britain headed ' L'Angleterre de Maggie la Terrible'. Her leadership was described as composed of 'charme' and 'terreur'. But this leadership seems to fit perfectly and to suit the entire nation. At least this is the image of today's Britain which appears on the front pages of foreign newspapers and on foreign television screens. This country, after the ending of the long imperial dream, goes out for excitement and for action. The British lion is not sleepwalking anymore. The violent scenes of the miners' strike, the war in the Falklands and Northern Ireland terrorism are the new pictures of Britain that are vividly in the minds of people overseas. They are the 'terreur'. At the same time Britain projects an innocent, gracious sort of charm with the smiles of Princess Diana, the sexy models, the new colourful fashions. This combination very much reflects the character of its ruler Mrs Thatcher.

Foreigners are mightily impressed by the Prime Minister's style of government. Once she has made a decision, they say, you may rest absolutely assured that it will be implemented, like it or not. None of that 'British pragmatism', so frequently shown to be nothing more than a bewildering series of U-turns, for her. Mrs Thatcher has so far refused to acknowledge the dictum that politics is the art of the possible. She seems not to worry about political risks and appears to be serenely unaffected by popularity polls. Seen from abroad, Mrs Thatcher appears to base her policies on faith. Other (perhaps lesser) politicians canvass their supporters, modifying their plans accordingly, testing the water, propitiating the gods, but this is not Mrs Thatcher's style. She is regarded abroad as a crusader, in the powerful tradition of Churchill, de Gaulle and Queen Victoria. Even if Mr Kinnock should win the next General Election, he will not be able to get away from Thatcher's legacy of a patriotic and industrious Britain. Fellow members of the European Community may complain that her quest – rock-solid financial accounting for Britain – often runs contrary to broader Community interests, but after six years of her leadership of Britain they are largely resigned to the fact that she does not intend to budge. A senior French diplomat was quoted in *The Sunday Times* (25 March 1984) as saying: 'That woman is an old-fashioned nationalist with no feeling for the European ideal. She reckons merely in terms of accountancy, not the broader political vision that is needed.'

Foreign politicians may jump up and down for the benefit of the press but there is a strong underlying current of admiration. In Europe she is infinitely better-known than Chancellor Kohl, President Mitterrand or Prime Minister Craxi, all of whom pale into insignificance beside her. She is an international celebrity, a political star. Like Talleyrand, she has restored her country to its pre-war mover-and-shaker status, not financially secure perhaps, but politically aggressive and influential.

No other European country would have gone to war for the Falklands, Not a single other Western European leader could have rallied his country into such an undertaking at such short notice and in the teeth of daunting logistical problems. The only politician since Churchill with such charisma was de Gaulle, which may be why Jacques Chirac goes on repeating, 'Elle est magnifique! Elle est comme le Général!' Lady Falkender has observed that following the Falklands victory Mrs Thatcher took to wearing higher heels. The *Economist* envisaged the Thatcher nose assuming the imperial proportions of the General's. Proboscis apart, there are certain similarities between the man who identified himself with France and the woman who aims, like Queen Victoria, to be the mother of the nation – to the dismay of Her Majesty Queen Elizabeth II. She believes in her mission to govern with 'love, care and firmness'. This does sound rather governessy and lacks the sweeping theatricality of de Gaulle's 'grandeur de la France'. But their aims, however couched, are identical: 'glory, glory, glory to the nation'. The General scored high marks in history books for statesmanship and patriotism, and Mrs Thatcher has already accomplished the same in an astonishingly short time.

Foreigners are naturally less concerned with British political squabbling about figures for industrial production, inflation, employment and the strength of the pound. Few people in Europe believe that Britain is only a whisker away from an economic miracle – but that is

irrelevant. The precise level of the pound against the
dollar is not of great interest to most Europeans, but, as
they once watched de Gaulle's posturings with mounting
irritation, so do they now exchange grumpy remarks
about Mrs Thatcher's Britain-first stance at Community
summits. Even the Italian Foreign Secretary, Signor
Giulio Andreotti, normally a Thatcher fan, was once
moved to make an uncharacteristically surly remark – he
compared her to 'a mean landlady who wants to be paid
in advance'.

There was a certain amount of sympathetic sniggering
among European leaders when former Prime Minister
Edward Heath referred to Mrs Thatcher's economics as
'the economics of the kitchen sink'. The European press,
however, are rather more inclined to sketch her in a
bellicose posture in direct contrast to Mr Heath's flaccid
domesticity. *Der Spiegel*, the German weekly, ran a cover
depicting the roaring British lion wearing Mrs Thatcher's face. The defiant image was echoed by the *Nouvel
Observateur*: 'Cette femme vit dans un bunker.'

The Americans too, have been known to get tetchy. No
one in Britain is likely to forget the criticisms voiced by
Mrs Jeanne Kirkpatrick in the United Nations General
Assembly during the Falklands war. At the same time
there was a newspaper report, never denied by the White
House, that President Reagan, in the course of a con-
versation with his then Secretary of State Alexander
Haig, said, 'That woman is looking for a skirmish.' In
fact, because of the arcane tenets of the Monroe Doc-
trine, America's leaders were perforce in a somewhat
tricky position during the Falklands war. As the undis-
puted leaders of the Western Hemisphere, the Americans
could not risk being on non-speaking terms with their
neighbours to the south. Similarly, extremely powerful

Irish-American politicians in the US Congress, such as Teddy Kennedy and Tip O'Neill, cannot risk the wrath of their constituents by having anything nice to say about the Prime Minister – her Northern Ireland policy is not exactly calibrated to Irish-American voters. That is not, as she says, her problem. For Irish-American politicians to condone violence would be foolish; for them to condemn the IRA would be political suicide; so they try to steer an uneasy course down the middle.

Fortunately for Mrs Thatcher and, by extension, for Great Britain, President Reagan's admiration is both unabashed and on record: 'Mrs Thatcher is the strongest man in Britain.' Well, that's certainly clear enough, although not a patch on the rich metaphorical tradition of the mysterious East: 'She is made from wolves and king cobras,' as the Hanoi newspaper *Quan Doi Nhan Dan* said. What the gentlemen from Hanoi have had no chance to experience is Mrs Thatcher's secret weapon – charm, and masses of it. President Reagan has been at Ground Zero and appears to be feeling the after-shock. As any *femme fatale* can tell you, charm is simply a matter of giving the charmee your undivided attention. Nothing new or startling there, one might think, but it's a rare and precious flower in the hands of a world leader. De Gaulle had a breadth of vision which the uncharitable called *folie de grandeur*, but he listened to no one; Eden was too aristocratic; Giscard d'Estaing too glacial; Jack Kennedy too, er, busy. But Mrs Thatcher has oodles of charm and uses great blasts of it. President Mitterrand, whose image is somewhat austere, was once quoted as saying that the 'divine' Margaret has 'les yeux de Caligula et la bouche de Marilyn Monroe'. Contrast that with Mr Denis Healey's pronouncement in *Penthouse*: 'She can lead the Tory party because she reminds the average public schoolboy of childhood fantasies – matron, and the enigmatic Miss Floggie! You know, long patent leather boots, a whip and a black corset!'

It is perfectly clear that the Prime Minister enjoys being considered an attractive woman with a dash of romantic sex appeal. The Mayor of Berlin once likened her to 'a beautiful rose'. Taking things a step or two further (as Italians are so very apt to do), the President of the Italian Republic, Signor Francesco Cossiga, when Prime Minister, achieved most-favoured-nation status with Mrs Thatcher through copious flower-sending, hand-kissing and dress-complimenting. In stark contrast, Monsieur Giscard d'Estaing was extremely aloof – perhaps, in fairness, any dress not made in Paris was invisible to him – and Chancellor Schmidt invariably appeared to be too busy listening to himself talk. No flowers from him!

In addition to her charm, Mrs Thatcher has also paid close attention to her own image to enhance Britain's prestige in the international community. Her clothes are perfect for her age and position. She has created for herself a sartorial niche between the respectable frumpiness of the Queen and the unreal, fairytale iridescence of the Princess of Wales. Her wardrobe tells the world in the language of silk and wool that Britain is solid and dependable *and* stylish, without frittering away national assets on extravagance à la Nancy Reagan.

Signor Giovanni Agnelli, president of Fiat (a state within a state) and himself a paragon of refined taste, has made no secret of his undying admiration for Mrs Thatcher and her role as an image-maker for Great Britain:

Mrs Thatcher represents a remarkable turning-point for

Europe. We Europeans have watched Britain waking up from her long sleep. For a long time Britain has shown a lack of willingness to pursue its economic and political goals. The so-called 'British disease' of inefficiency spread across the Channel and affected other European nations. Mrs Thatcher has changed the image of Britain. She is a Prime Minister with courage and resolution and she has set an example which has been of great help to us on the Continent.

Many Italian statesmen are poetic in their praise for Mrs Thatcher. Signor Craxi, the Prime Minister, says, 'Sometimes when arguing with Maggie, I feel liverish. But I find her attractive and stimulating. One cannot help admiring her for her ferocious defence of British interests abroad.' The former President of the Italian Republic, Signor Pertini, has confessed to dreaming of 'waltzing with the beautiful lady'. The Foreign Secretary, Signor Guilio Andreotti, who had personal experience of how the Iron Lady can be brusque with her guests and who tried to insist on a matter in which she had already made up her mind, said:

> I tried to put to Mrs Thatcher the idea, which I had already discussed with the French Foreign Secretary, Claude Cheysson, of the reopening of the negotiations about the future of the Falklands and she cut me dead. I had the impression that she felt that it was almost an insult to her to mention this.

Above all else, Margaret Thatcher has become, in the eyes of the world, the mirror of her country. Not the chaotic Britain of the 1960s and 1970s but a reversion to a much earlier concept of what the country is all about. A nation of shopkeepers? Yes, partly that, without being ashamed of it, for Mrs Thatcher makes no bones about being a shopkeeper's daughter. She affects none of the languid insouciance of the aristocracy. Her speeches are clear and her accent, brought down a tone for television on the advice of media expert Gordon Reece, is now a fair approximation of upper-middle-class – certainly more so than Mr Heath's. Any Americanisms used by her are in audible inverted commas, unlike the popular and toadying mid-Atlantic accent that was once so favoured by politicians.

Mr Healey, in the *Penthouse* interview quoted earlier, was trying to explain away Mrs Thatcher's success in blatantly class-conscious terms ('She can lead the Tory party because she reminds *the average public schoolboy* of childhood fantasies . . . '); he cannot actually believe that the Tory Party is composed entirely of public schoolboys. The people who have twice voted Mrs Thatcher into leading the nation are precisely the same nation of shopkeepers at which Napoleon sneered. They are Mrs Thatcher and she is one of them.

The political emphasis of the 1960s and 1970s was also a reflection of British society. The focus was on youth – on youthful ideals and youthful iconoclasm. MPs listened with at least an outward show of respect to the political philosophies of students. France ground to a halt in 1968 when its universities went to the barricades. Jack Kennedy started the Peace Corps and Carnaby Street spawned a fashion industry that was virtually Britain's best-known foreign currency earner. If you couldn't actually *be* young you had to make an effort to think young. How things have changed in the 1980s! The President of the United States is elderly by any standard and the spring chicken among the world's leaders is the leader of the Soviet Union. The mood of the Western world has swung towards middle age – middle-aged disillusionment, middle-aged conformity and middle-aged repressiveness, leavened perhaps by a dash of middle-aged pragmatism. This is the mood that has voted in and supports the 1980s Britannia, a strong and authoritative lady resolved to re-create the glory of the days of the British Empire, and who, by being in step with the times, has captured the imagination of the entire Western world.

No more telling postscript could be found than the fact that in Italy Signorina Cinza Carosio, a successful travel agent, has started to sell the 'Thatcher Itinerary', in the same way that travel agencies sell pilgrimages to the places where Christ was born, educated and crucified. The Thatcher pilgrimage consists of travelling to Grantham, and having lunch at the Premier Restaurant there, vising Somerville College in Oxford, her Finchley constituency and the Palace of Westminster, getting a glimpse of Downing Street and then, as a finale, paying a visit to Flood Street in Chelsea where she used to live. One might fairly conclude that the apotheosis of Margaret Thatcher, today's Britannia, is complete.

Select Bibliography

Barzini, Luigi, *From Caesar to the Mafia*, The Library Press, New York, 1971.

Blow, Simon, *Fields Elysian, A Portrait of Hunting Society*, Dent, London, 1983.

Brittan, Samuel, *Capitalism and the Permissive Society*, Macmillan, London, 1973.

Buckle, Richard, *U & Non-U Revisited*, Futura, London, 1978.

Burke, Thomas, *The Streets of London Through the Centuries*, Charles Scribner's Sons, New York, 1941.

Butler, Eamonn, *Hayek: His Contribution to the Political and Economic Thought of Our Time*, Temple Smith, London, 1983.

Compton Miller, *Who's Really Who*, Sphere Books Ltd, London, 1983.

Cosgrave, Patrick, *Thatcher, The First Term*, Bodley Head, London, 1985.

Daninos, Pierre, *Snobissimo*, Librairie Hachette, Paris, 1964.

Darwin, Bernard, *British Clubs*, Collins, London, 1957.

Davey, Richard, *The Pageant of London*, Methuen & Co., London, 1906.

Davis, William, *The Rich: A Study of the Species*, Sidgwick & Jackson, London, 1982.

Della Torre, Paolo Filo, *Thatcher La Bambola Di Ferro*, Rizzoli, Milan, 1983.

99

100 *Viva Britannia*

Dullar, Philippa, *Gilded Butterflies: The Rise and Fall of the London Season*, Hamish Hamilton, London, 1978.

Franzero, Carlo Maria, *Cinquant'anni a Londra*, Societa Editirice Internazionale, Torino, 1975.

Garrucio, Ludovico, *Italia Senza Eroi*, Rusconi, Milan, 1980.

Ghirelli, Antonio, *L'Effetto Craxi*, Rizzoli, Milan, 1982.

Keegan, William, *Mrs Thatcher's Economic Experiment*, Allen Lane, London, 1984.

Lacey, Robert, *Aristocrats*, Hutchinson/BBC Publications, London, 1983.

Lippi, Lorenzo, *Il Malmantile Racquistato*, Antonio Zatta e Figli, 1938.

Lowry, Suzanne, *Young Fogey Handbook*, Javelin Books, Blandford, Dorset, 1985.

Mankowitz, Wolf, *Dickens of London*, Weidenfeld & Nicolson, London, 1976.

Mikes, George, *How to be a Brit*, André Deutsch, London, 1984.

Pearce, Edward, *The Senate of Lilliput*, Faber and Faber, London, 1983.

Pelling, Henry, *Origins of the Labour Party*, Oxford University Press, Oxford, 1965.

Phillips, Pearson, *The Complete Guide to Young Aspiring Professionals*, Arrow Books, London, 1984.

Piazzesi, Gianfranco, *L'Italia Spiegata Al Popolo*, Rizzoli, Milan, 1977.

Priestley, J.B., *The English*, Heinemann, London, 1973.

Quennel, Peter, *Byron: The Years of Fame*, Collins, London, 1943.

Ramsden, John, *The Making of Conservative Party Policy: The Conservative Research Department Since 1939*, Longman, London, 1980.

Ramsden, John, *Real Old Tory Politics: The Political Diaries of Robert Sanders, Lord Bayford 1910–1935*, The Historians' Press, 1984.

Rose, Richard, *Studies in British Politics*, Macmillan, London, 1966.

Sampson, Anthony, *Anatomy of Britain*, Hodder & Stoughton, London, 1982.

Seldon, Arthur, *Rebirth of Britain: A Symposium of Essays by Eighteen Writers*, Pan Books Ltd, London, 1964.

Williams, Marcia, *Inside Number 10*, Weidenfeld & Nicolson, London, 1972.

Woods, Maurice, *The History of the Tory Party*, Hodder & Stoughton, London, 1924.

York, Peter and Ann Barr, *The Official Sloane Ranger's Diary*, Ebury Press, London, 1983.